RIHANNA

RIHANNA

the unauthorized biography

DANNY WHITE

Michael O'Mara Books Limited

First published in Great Britain in 2013 by
Michael O'Mara Books Limited
9 Lion Yard
Tremadoc Road
London SW4 7NQ

A CIP catalogue record for this book is available from the British Library.

Papers used by Michael O'Mara Books Limited are natural, recyclable
products made from wood grown in sustainable forests. The
manufacturing processes conform to the environmental regulations of
the country of origin.

ISBN: 978-1-78243-047-6 in trade paperback print format
ISBN: 978-1-78243-049-0 in EPub format
ISBN: 978-1-78243-050-6 in Mobipocket format

1 2 3 4 5 6 7 8 9 10

Designed and typeset by Ana Bjezancevic
Printed and bound by CPI Group (UK) Ltd, Croydon, CR0 4YY

www.mombooks.com

Contents

Introduction

What complex creatures superstars are. If you closely examine any of the hallowed few at the pinnacle of fame you will uncover a heady mass of contradictions, and no star of the modern age is more contradictory than Robyn Rihanna Fenty. She is at once imperious and beaten; controlling and submissive; her image simultaneously sexually charged and charmingly innocent. She carefully manipulates and revels in her media notoriety, but the price she has had to pay has broken her heart. Since the very start of her career, the sassy songbird has positioned herself as the devil-may-care, rebel artist of pop, yet her committed, industrious work rate goes beyond that of an obsessive, prompting one commentator to wonder whether she is, in fact, a robot.

The contradictory atmosphere continues into her music itself. While the lyrics of her hits are frequently concerned with the most adult of themes – including domestic violence and sadomasochistic sex – their musical charm is often deliberately childlike. With an 'ella, ella' here, and an 'ooh na na' there, she has made global smash hits out of songs whose musical structure is the same as nursery rhymes. Indeed, even her most controversial hit, 'S&M', reworked a children's rhyme into an X-rated celebration of sadomasochism. Rihanna, who once said she wanted to become 'the black Madonna', certainly shares the material girl's love of extremes, reinventions and mixed messages.

Well, it works for us. The Barbadian had, as of 2012, sold 8.7 million albums in the US alone, and 58 million songs via downloads. She has had more US number one hits – twelve – than Whitney Houston did in her entire career. She has won six GRAMMY Awards, three MTV Video Music Awards, five American Music Awards, eighteen Billboard Music Awards – and all this before she turned twenty-five years old. The media cannot get enough of her: thanks in part to the darkly fascinating Chris Brown saga, she generated 10,355 headlines in 2012 alone, according to *Forbes* magazine. She is keenly followed on social networks including Twitter, where she has over 27 million followers, and was the first female artist to attract 2 billion views on YouTube, outstripping even Lady Gaga.

Yet how she delights in mystifying us. She is the pop industry's chief chameleon; somehow able to make radical changes to her appearance and image with ostensibly minor adjustments. A natural tease, she has kept us on the edge of our seats for years.

Here is the real Rihanna.

1.

Life Before Fame

'I had a life before my record deal,' said Rihanna in 2007. And what a life it was. Her early years were dramatic and character-building; they provided ample opportunity for her to go off the rails, and yet somehow Rihanna remained fundamentally on course. Her childhood was played out under the dark shadow of her father's dependence on class-A drugs, fierce domestic violence within the family home, and her resultant self-doubt and health difficulties. Yet, to hear her talk sometimes, it would be easy to get a very different impression of her early years. 'It was perfect, really,' she told *Interview* magazine, for instance. She has been more candid elsewhere. In a separate interview she said, 'My tough childhood made me the person I am today.' In reality, hers was a childhood of stark contrasts: one of austerity, tests and torment amid surroundings that were close to blissful.

Robyn Rihanna Fenty was born on 20 February 1988 at the Queen Elizabeth Hospital on the island of Barbados. Her parents were Ronald Fenty, then a warehouse supervisor for a garment manufacturer, and Monica Braithwaite, then an accountant. Monica's mother had moved to Barbados from Guyana. Ronald's forebears included Irish settlers, yet it was his stepfather who had the greatest impact on him as he grew up. He had beaten young Ronald, whose vulnerability was intensified by the fact his mother did not intervene.

These experiences left a weighty mark on Ronald's life and it has been speculated that this maternal failing filled him with resentment towards women, thus igniting the furious fire in him that led to him beating Monica after they married. It is also highly likely that this cycle of abuse was, unhappily, something Ronald was unable to break, a difficulty faced by many victims of familial violence.

Ronald met Monica when they were both high school students. At first they were just good friends; in time they became lovers. Pertinently, at the age of fourteen, Ronald was already taking drugs including cannabis and, most perilously, the hugely addictive crack cocaine. As the couple did not wed until 1985, when they were both in their thirties, Monica entered the marriage under no illusions at all that her partner had serious issues with drug addiction. She tried hard to see the man himself as separate to the addiction, but he would regularly test her patience to its very limits. Indeed, Ronald's drug problem and its bitter consequences became known by many in the neighbourhood. According to *The Sun*, some onlookers dubbed Ronald a 'parrow' – a disparaging local colloquialism meaning a freeloading drug addict. This was not the only tittle-tattle the pair attracted: they also faced prejudicial glances and comments over the fact that theirs was a mixed-race marriage. Further, when the newlywed couple did not have a baby during the first three years of their marriage, some locals gossiped to the effect that Ronald's drug use had left him sterile.

In fact, Ronald had three children from a previous marriage, so the infertility rumours were incorrect – Rihanna actually has two half-sisters and a half-brother. She met one of her half-sisters, Kandy, when she was fifteen years of age and Kandy also introduced Rihanna to her own two daughters, Brandy and Crystal. Her nieces took to Rihanna from the moment they first met. Another of her half-sisters, Samantha, noted their similarities, describing Rihanna as 'a mini-me'. After three years of marriage, the birth of Ronald and Monica's first child nailed the infertility rumour, and Rihanna was soon joined by two younger brothers. Rorrey was born in November 1990, and Rajad in April 1997. As the eldest of the family's offspring – with nine years separating her and her youngest sibling – Rihanna is, according to those who subscribe to 'birth-order' theories, expected to have a nurturing, organized and compassionate nature. Another characteristic common among eldest siblings is an enhanced ability to communicate. The theory is that they will have heard more adult conversations during their formative years than their subsequent siblings. A tendency for people-pleasing is also believed to be ubiquitous among firstborns, as they have often been hurt by losing the undivided attention of their parents at an early age, and then work hard to get it back. Some would say that public performers are inherently people-pleasers, driven by a need for approval, particularly the warmth of applause.

Born under the star sign of Pisces, Rihanna is further believed, in astrological circles at least, to have a tendency to be imaginative, sensitive, creative and highly intuitive. Pisceans are also thought to be most comfortable working for themselves or at the head of a team. Other famous Pisceans include Queen Latifah, Aretha Franklin, Rupert Murdoch and Kurt Cobain – a varied bunch of celebrity names to say the least. (There is evidence that Rihanna believes in astrology. After she partied the night away with strippers in the spring of 2012, she retweeted a comment about Pisceans having 'the most active sexual fantasy life'. A more direct symbol of her belief is the fish she has tattooed behind her right ear – generally regarded to be an explicit tribute to her astrological sign.)

*

The Fenty family lived on Westbury New Road in a modest three-bedroom bungalow. Westbury New Road is in Bridgetown, the island's capital city and commercial centre, which lies within the parish of Saint Michael. With a population of just 80,000 people, Bridgetown is a relatively small capital city. However, it is the commercial hub of the island and home to its parliament buildings on Broad Street. As for Barbados itself, Rihanna describes it as 'very proper and conservative'. Although she has long left the island, these attitudes remain relevant to her life and career to this day: frequently, her conservative countrymen have looked on with disapproval at the increasingly raunchy image of Barbados's famous female pop export.

Her childhood home may have been a modest building, but it was set in a desirable location – just thirty metres away from the dazzling coastline. Indeed, her home's proximity to the beach made Rihanna feel that she was growing up in 'paradise', and that she was 'on vacation' every day. Her surroundings were definitely bordering on the blissful, as was the climate of the island. Her childhood was testing in several senses, yet it was only after she left Barbados in her mid-teens that she realized just how fortunate she was to have been raised in such an exotic location.

As she looks back she recognizes that she took considerable advantage of its delights. 'We really took it for granted, but we basically spent the entire day on the beach with summer all year round,' she said. 'It wasn't special to us because that was just normal for Barbados.' Her happiest memories of her childhood include learning to swim, catching fish and crabs at the beach and learning how to ride a bike. 'It's funny, because most of these times were with my dad,' she told the *Guardian*.

She describes her childhood district as a 'slightly less than average neighbourhood', elaborating: 'It wasn't the poorest, and it definitely wasn't the richest.' She agrees that the culture of Barbados has had a significant influence on her character and her life. It toughened her up, for instance. 'The way we are with each other in Barbados – it really helped to have a thick skin, coming from Barbados,' she once told ITV's *Daybreak*.

She was teased from an early age over her mixed-race heritage, or for 'being a bi-racial', as she puts it. She was also sometimes told she was an 'ugly pig'. This taunting was just the first of the tests that life threw at her as a child – 'If it wasn't one thing, it was another thing,' she said. But things would get a lot worse before they got better.

Meanwhile, as she tried her best to find her place in a world she found so strange, she also began to develop and assert her own identity. One early memory concerns the time when the four-year-old Rihanna quietly borrowed Monica's nail varnish. However, it was not her nails that she planned to use it on. Instead, she used it to paint bangle shapes on her arms, tipping the remainder of the varnish over a hat belonging to Rorrey. No wonder then that when Monica realized what had happened she was very angry, particularly as there was no varnish remover in the household. A part of her could not wait until her daughter began her education.

The first school Rihanna attended was the Charles F. Broome Memorial School, a primary school around half a mile away from the family home. She also attended religious services officiated by Bishop Vibert Lowe. It was at these services that she became increasingly enchanted by the power of music. Nowadays, she is at odds with the church due to her raunchy image and wild personal life, but it was the church that first opened her ears to the simple yet powerful beauty of song.

Ronald remembers when he first heard his daughter sing: she was three years old and lying on her bed, holding a hairbrush in her hands as an improvised microphone. The classic Whitney Houston ballad 'Saving All My Love For You' was one of the songs she would perform as her love of music grew. There was little out of the ordinary about this at first; children around the world perform hairbrush-wielding 'concerts' in their bedrooms. Yet by the time she was six, she was already forming an ambition to become a professional singer.

Ronald remembers hearing her sing when she was seven, and this time he noticed something special. 'I heard her singing with our neighbour and I was amazed,' he told *The Sun*. 'She was doing the *Aladdin* song "A Whole New World" – it was so pretty I couldn't believe it.' He wondered whether his daughter had inherited her 'angelic singing' voice from his own parents, both of whom were talented vocalists. He noticed that, as well as singing impressively, she was a naturally gifted dancer, 'but she wasn't doing all the school productions and stuff'.

Dawn Johnson, who lived next door to the family, also heard Rihanna sing. 'We used to call her Robyn Red Breast because she was always singing like a bird,' she told *The Sun*. 'We are so close we could hear her singing from the bathroom.' Across the road was Shakira Pilgrim, a girl with whom Rihanna would become good friends. By all accounts the pair were inseparable as kids. As well as performing impromptu mini 'concerts' for her neighbours to hear, Rihanna also loved listening to music. In keeping with Bajan culture, her playlists included lots of reggae. Such rhythms were inescapable on the island; they were the very soundtrack of her childhood. 'Reggae was standard, you always listen to reggae in Barbados,' she explained later. One of her favourite tracks was 'No Woman, No Cry' by Bob Marley & The Wailers. She also adored soul music, particularly the big-voiced, big-named stars of the genre. Asked who were her favourites she replied, 'The divas: Whitney Houston, Celine Dion, Mariah Carey, Shania Twain. I loved Luther Vandross. Still love him.' The more she listened, the more she began to understand – instinctively at first – what it is that goes into making a great song.

Indeed, music played an increasingly central part in her life as she moved into adolescence. Prior to her teenage years, she had been quite a studious child. She loved books and could often be found reading. She describes herself then as nerdy, '*too* nerdy', in fact. But, gradually, the bookish side of her was being superseded by a more knowing and sassy personality. Indeed, the teenage girl who would eventually emerge from so many testing times was a surprisingly well adjusted and philosophical one. Her childhood has given her a rational perspective on life. 'Minor things don't bother me,' she said. Indeed, if Rihanna was to take one lesson from her childhood, it would be this: 'You get what you put in, and that has stuck with me.'

It would be tempting to speculate that it was only music that helped her cope with the challenges of her childhood. However, she had help to that end from her mother. Indeed, Rihanna has said that, thanks to the way Monica raised her children, they were never aware of their impoverished circumstances. 'My mom never made us feel that way,' she told *Glamour*. 'She made us feel that anything was possible and instilled in me such confidence.' She told TV chanel Bravo, 'It wasn't all great in my childhood, but there are a lot of positive memories as well and I have to thank my mom for them.'

Describing Monica as 'one of the strongest women I know, if not the strongest', she credits her mother for raising her 'in a way that I could be responsible and fearless', adding, 'She made me realize that it comes with consequences.'

There is a strong sense that Rihanna is wise beyond her years, and, again, it is a quality that she credits Monica for instilling in her. 'My mom raised me to be a child and know my place but also to think like a woman. She never held back from me in terms of being too young to know certain things, so I am very mature for my age.' The influence was all-pervading: even today, Rihanna catches herself mirroring Monica's mannerisms, particularly her facial expressions. Nowadays this makes her feel proud and fond, but when she was a child and people pointed out their similarity she was, naturally, less pleased. It is a rare child who wants to be compared to their parent. 'Oh gross, *never*,' she would protest, every inch the petulant child craving her own independent identity.

Rihanna was always something of a tomboy. At school she found it hard to make friends, particularly with girls. 'I didn't get along with people very well,' she told *Interview*. 'I got along with guys, but I hated the girls and the teachers.' As a result of this, her social circle was dominated by young males. 'My mother didn't understand that for a long time. There were all these different guys calling the house, and she probably had a totally different idea of what was happening.' The fact that she spent so much time in male company has left a lasting influence on her character, perhaps helping to shape the assured, borderline feisty, part of her image that is so popular among her fans today.

As a child, her self-assurance helped Rihanna to develop an entrepreneurial streak. She used to join her father as he sold clothes and other items on a street stall. 'She'd come outside of the store and put up a rack and sell hats and belts and scarves,' Ronald told *The Sun*. He added that she also went into business at school, buying loose sweets from the local shop and then packing them up to sell to her school friends at a tasty mark-up. For all her drive and tomboyish side, Rihanna did not lack femininity. She liked wearing pink – an early photograph shows her wearing a pink shirt as she poses alongside Rorrey outside the family home – and she wore the colour so often that she was nicknamed 'Miss Pinky' by family and friends. Although she felt unhappy with her appearance, she had no need to. Her cousin Nicola Alleyne's recollections of the future star's appearance back then are admiring: 'I just remember her curly hair and beautiful eyes.' Speaking to the *Daily Mail* of her cousin's personality, Alleyne added: 'She was a really determined person. When she set herself on something she would just do it. She's stubborn and sticks to her guns. She's just a very likeable person.'

This sense of a restless, vivacious character is enhanced by the recollections of another of her cousins, Amanda Thompson. 'I used to plait her hair,' Thompson proudly told the *Daily Mail*. 'I used to plait everyone's hair in the family. Rihanna would never stay quiet for ten seconds. She was special then and she's special now.'

Another relative with whom Rihanna was close as a child was her maternal grandmother, Clara 'Dolly' Braithwaite, whom she affectionately nicknamed GranGran Dolly. Only after her grandmother died in 2012 did Rihanna begin to share details of their bond, posting on Twitter photographs of her, as a child, alongside her grandmother. She also shared with the world a picture of some teddy bears she had once given her grandmother as a present. She was touched that Braithwaite had kept them. During Rihanna's childhood their bond was strong: it was her grandmother who coined Rihanna's nickname, 'Rebel Flower', a name that sums up well the two sides of both her childhood and her personality.

However, Rihanna would need every bit of the confidence that Monica had handed her and all of the toughness that her male friends offered as two dark shadows were cast across her childhood. Starting when she was eight years old, Rihanna began to suffer from terrible headaches – the pain was crippling at times.

The problem continued for six years, into her teenage years, by which time her parents feared she might have a tumour, and she underwent a series of CAT (computed axial tomography) scans. 'It was that intense,' recalled Rihanna. Nothing physical was found to be wrong with her and it was only later, looking back, that she formed the opinion that the headaches were brought on by the enormous stress she was under due to discord in the family home. Although they eased during her teenage years, they have struck her afresh more recently, as we shall see.

Along with the headaches, she also began to become intensely conscious of her own appearance. Dissatisfied by her slender physique, Rihanna wanted a curvy body like her mother's. However much she was told that her shape would change as she got older, she continued to dream of a different body, hoping she could have 'triangular' thighs like Monica's. She still often wishes for a different body but she has learned to accept that such desires are a part of life.

Behind these crises of confidence was the domestic discord prompted by her father's continued use of drugs. According to Chloe Govan in her book *Rihanna: Rebel Flower*, since the early years of Rihanna's life her father would often disappear from the family home for days on end. He was, in truth, hiding in body and mind: he would take drugs with fiery enthusiasm during his absences. It is worth pausing to consider and understand the effect that crack cocaine in particular has on the user who can become instantly and grievously addicted to it from the very first high. This smokeable form of cocaine, which first came into existence during the 1960s, offers an instant and intense 'hit'. The flipside of this is that the 'comedown' or 'crash' afterwards is swift and savage, leaving users feeling enormously depressed and, consequently, desperate for their next 'fix'. Suddenly, addicts are unable to concentrate on anything other than maintaining a regular supply of the drug.

Ronald's lengthy absences left Monica having to work even harder just to keep the family financially afloat. As Rihanna later put it, her mother was having to be the woman and the man of the household, 'working her ass off for us'. But if Ronald's absences caused problems for the family then his presence could be even more difficult. The way that Rihanna describes her childhood awareness of Ronald's drug addiction is heartbreaking. 'Even as a child, I would learn that my mom and dad would argue when there was foil paper in the ashtray,' she told the *Mirror*, offering a chilling glimpse into the way children symbolically understand such adult torment. 'He would just go into the bathroom all the time. I didn't know what it was.'

Sometimes, she noticed 'marijuana and cocaine

around him' but at the time she did not know what these substances were, or the harm they were causing to her parents' marriage. 'I just knew that my mom didn't like it, and they were always fighting about it.' It was as Ronald 'came down' from the high that he would become particularly volatile. It made for a terrifying household. 'I was out of control,' he told *The Sun*. 'I would let my wife and children down time and time again. I was not a good dad or husband.' Even though Monica did her best to shield the children from what was going on, it was tricky to do so when she was out of the house working such long hours.

Rihanna felt confused and conflicted by it all. As she later told *The Observer*, 'A child shouldn't have to go through that. Being in the whirlwind, it frustrates you, it angers you, because you're being tortured and you don't know why.' Nowadays she is open about what happened inside the family home as she grew up. However, at the time she kept her lips sealed. Indeed, children in abusive households often keep the cause of their pain hidden. She believed that this tendency was exacerbated in Barbados where, she said of familial tensions, 'We keep it in our family and figure it out and move on.' Therefore, she added, 'domestic violence is a big secret.' It was an enormous burden for her to carry. It tested her ability as an elder sibling and meant that for many years her shoulders bore a heavy weight.

On one particularly harrowing and memorable day, Rihanna, then nine years of age, witnessed Ronald smoking crack. At this stage, her father had promised his wife that his drug use was a thing of the past. So when Rihanna secretly spotted him smoking, she faced the dilemma of whether to say anything to him, or to Monica. She decided that she had to tell her mother what she had seen. For Ronald, who only noticed at the last moment that he was being watched, this was a sobering moment. 'I instantly came back down from the high I was on,' he told *The Sun*. 'I saw her run for her mother, [tell] her something and then they both started to cry.' He added, 'It was the lowest point – life just stopped and I realized what a fool I had been.'

Nonetheless, it was around this time that her parents first separated, which thrust Rihanna, who had yet to reach double figures, into a quasi-parental role in the family. She was tasked with looking after her youngest brother, Rajad. 'My mom was a single mom, so she worked a lot. She was really never home – I mean, she was home, but it would be after work, late at night, so I would take care of him. He was my best friend. He thought I was his mom!'

For some time, Rihanna felt embittered towards Ronald for the way his drug use had broken up the family and forced her to become adult and wise before her time. It would have been scant consolation for her to realize that, actually, Ronald had been lucky throughout his crack use: the drug's instantaneous effects mean it carries a high risk of fatal overdose. Her anger was immense: indeed, she told the *Guardian* that she actually hated him for some time. 'Then, one of my school friends, who I was very close to, she knew, and she always used to say, "You can't hate your father," that you have to love him, at the end of the day, because he's your father. So I listened, as much as it took out of me.'

It was perhaps then that Rihanna's longstanding commitment to pursuing personal growth was born. Long before the abuse she herself suffered in a later relationship, the abuse she watched Ronald inflict on Monica and, as a consequence, the wider family, also made her resolve never to allow herself to be trapped in such a situation in her own life. 'I said to myself, "I'm never gonna date someone like my dad,"' she told ABC, adding: 'Never.' These words took on a chilling dimension in 2009.

However, back then, a subsequent symbolic moment was enough, Ronald has claimed, to sober him up. The family were out walking one day when they saw a 'down and out' sleeping on the pavement. Monica turned to Rihanna and said: 'Your dad is going to end up like that.' For Ronald, who had already noted that his little girl looked at him 'differently' because of his drug addiction, this was a chilling moment. 'I did not want my children to see me sleeping on the sidewalk so I started making the changes,' he told *The Sun*. 'I had to give up drugs for my family. I still kind of lost them, I split up with my wife. But I still had to do it for myself and eventually I beat it.' Before he reached 'eventually', Ronald continued to perturb the family.

When he returned to the family home, Rihanna was very unsettled by his renewed presence. She needed a positive distraction outside of this claustrophobic household and she eventually found one – in the unlikely shape of the Barbados Cadet Corps and its fearsome summer camp. Indeed, this was more of a challenge than a distraction, as the camp included a string of mentally and physically draining tests. This was a *real* boot camp, before reality television redefined that term as some sort of singing contest. As the organizers boast, the cadet programme is 'deliberately intense' with standards 'set very high'. The programme included an arduous initiation that saw Rihanna and her fellow cadets flung into the wilderness with only the most basic tools of survival. They were challenged to run, cycle and swim, while shooting and navigation were also firmly on the agenda.

Rihanna's friend Shontelle Layne was also at the camp, where she held the rank of drill sergeant. She has since invited viewers of the BBC Entertainment channel to imagine herself and Rihanna 'in combat boots and fatigues crawling through mud and things like that'. It certainly makes for a diverting image. Layne also had to issue orders to Rihanna. 'That's what drill sergeants do,' she explained. 'We boss cadets around, we make them do push-ups – especially when they show up on the parade square late.' Layne added, 'She used to be late all the time because she was in the bathroom making sure her lip gloss was sparkly.' Despite her tardiness, Rihanna often surprised the camp with her determination and ability. On her arrival, in the eyes of many, her blossoming good looks and attention to her own appearance marked her out as one unlikely to thrive. However, she did well in many of the challenges, particularly impressing in compass reading and shooting. Indeed, the care and pride she took in her appearance was an advantage in one aspect of the camp. As Layne told *Hollywood Life*, 'In cadet camp, your appearance is important.' Given that marks were given for a neat appearance, Rihanna's natural tendency to present herself well helped. 'She was a really good cadet,' said Layne. Rihanna was such a striking figure that Layne felt, even back then, that she could go on to become famous as a model. Her star quality was already starting to shine, even amid such unglamorous surroundings. As for Rihanna herself, she said she has 'dreamed of being a cover girl since I was a little girl'. She recalls being 'fascinated' as she watched Monica apply her make-up.

The cadet camp had proved just the sort of confidence-building experience she needed. Her best friend, Melissa Forde, was another keen influence on Rihanna's growing assurance. They met when Rihanna was fourteen, and her new friend quickly influenced our heroine's personality and self-image, both of which became not just more confident, but also more feminine. The tomboyish Rihanna of old began to give way to a more girlie character. She had noticed Melissa from the moment she joined the school – 'She really stood out,' Rihanna said. Immediately, the pair 'just clicked', leading to a sharp increase in determination and poise for Rihanna.

Her bolder and more streetwise mood was reflected in her dress. She made a point of bucking the trends that so many of her friends were anxiously following. As she would later tell style bible *Vogue*, 'When I was fourteen and first started going out, I always wanted to be the opposite of everyone else. So I would go to the club in a polo t-shirt and pants and sneakers and a hat on backward, just so I would not be dressed like other girls.' All the time she was looking further and wider than her contemporaries, becoming ever more 'desperate for things that weren't available in Barbados'. To this end, she would enthusiastically clip photographs out of magazines, to keep a record of the sort of looks that captured her imagination. 'I was obsessed with creating a visual with clothing, and the way things are combined.'

She began to drink alcohol at a young age – by the time she was fourteen she was already going out drinking with her friends. She has suggested that this was not out of the ordinary among teenagers in Barbados. 'The country's pretty laid-back about the legal age for drinking,' she told the *Daily Mail*. Though she says she would 'get drunk', she insisted she 'never went over the top', adding, 'I wasn't exactly in the Amy Winehouse mode.' Although she made that statement before the troubled British singer died in 2011, Rihanna had already seen enough from Winehouse's at times chaotic lifestyle – and that of her own father – to be wary of surrendering herself to alcohol. 'I wasn't going to follow in his footsteps,' she said. 'I knew my limits when I was a kid.' To specify where her red line stood, she said she would not 'get to the point where I want to throw up, can't stand straight or say things I'm likely to regret in the morning'.

On many of those nights out, she would be paying attention to the guys – younger and older – at the clubs. She had, by this time, had her first encounter with the opposite sex. It was not an enjoyable one. 'My first kiss was in high school, and it was the worst thing ever,' she told *Rolling Stone*. 'He pretty much dumped his entire saliva glands into my mouth.' Recalling how the experience 'traumatized' her, she added that as a result she did not kiss again 'for, like, ever'. Friends, however, recall a different Rihanna: one who would be vying for the attention of men in nightclubs and who in time developed an unwarranted reputation as a 'slut'. This allegation would reappear when she became a famous singer.

The parochial attitudes of her neighbours only encouraged Rihanna to consider what wonders might lie beyond the island on which she lived. She began to dream of what could be possible if she took the energy, philosophy and determination she had used in her cadet camp and businesses and applied it to the musical aspirations she was forming in her mind. When she observed divas such as Whitney Houston, Janet Jackson and Destiny's Child, she was flushed with ambition. '[I thought] "I want to be like them, I want to do that one day, I want to back videos, make music and have CDs",' she told MTV. 'That started the dream and it just went from there, and became a reality.' When it eventually happened it made Rihanna arguably the biggest contemporary musical star to come from her region, at least on a par with the likes of Wyclef Jean of Haiti and Jamaica's Shaggy and Sean Paul.

The man who was to help her in her quest would enter her life on a fateful trip to Barbados.

2.

A Dream Come True

The reason Evan Rogers and Rihanna came to meet was that Rogers was married to a Bajan woman. The newlyweds went on holiday to Barbados and, thanks to his wife's local connections and Evan's passion and musical know-how, they were eagerly in touch with the local music scene. Thus it was that young Rihanna, whose voice and ambition was starting to become known among islanders, came under the radar of just the man who could turn her burgeoning dreams into a reality.

So, who is Evan Rogers?

Rogers and his friend Carl Sturken formed a band together in their younger years and also worked as session musicians, but it was as producers and songwriters that they would find fortune. Rogers is, predominantly, a lyrics man while Sturken often took care of the musical side. They were established in the industry long before their paths crossed with Rihanna, having masterminded the 1980s comeback of 1960s star Donny Osmond, working with girl group Eternal, boy bands 'N Sync and Boyzone, and pop solo stars including Christina Aguilera and Nick Jonas. They had also dipped their toes into the world of television, penning tracks for Kelly Clarkson and Ruben Studdard, the respective winners of the first two series of the Fox Television hit show *American Idol*. Following this track record of success over nearly three decades, they decided to build their own record label, rather than working for others. Their ambition and hunger were huge and their ability beyond doubt. Without an artist, though, their new label – SRP Records – was doomed to failure.

Rihanna was just the sort of young, raw talent they were after. Likewise, they were just the sort of talented and energetic industry figures that she needed to meet. She had formed a band with two friends, Jose Blackman and Kelenna Browne, and the trio were keen to make a proper go of things. With an eye on the importance of a distinctive image, they called themselves Contrast, to reflect the different racial backgrounds of each member. They also hoped the name would evoke a positive sense of the variety of people living in Barbados. Having each tasted the sourness of prejudice and suspicion, they hoped to bring some pride back to all the people of the island, whatever their background. The main focus was always the music, though. They would meet and rehearse at the weekend, singing songs by acts such as Mariah Carey and Destiny's Child.

Imagine their excitement when word came that a music producer who had already sold tens of millions of records wanted to audition them. Rihanna went to great lengths both to prepare the band for the key performance and also to find out whatever she could about the man auditioning them. To sense an opportunity ahead may not have required inate perception, but to fully grasp the enormity of it did. The band's moment of destiny was to take place at Rogers' villa at the luxurious Sandy Lane Hotel, which is set in a heavenly resort favoured by the rich and famous. Its tranquillity and ornate architecture have made it an increasingly popular destination since it opened in the early 1960s. Taking pride of place among this splendour was Rogers' villa – a spacious affair with all the trappings of success.

Rihanna was desperately nervous when she arrived for the audition. Finally, she felt, she had a chance of cracking into 'the big world that was so unreachable'. But that knowledge alone was enough to make her feel enormously anxious. However, her charisma and star quality had captured Rogers' attention before she even started singing. This would prove a mixed blessing for her: she was about to discover the advantage and disadvantage of having a star that shines brighter than that of others.

'The minute Rihanna walked into the room, it was like the other two girls didn't exist,' Rogers told *Entertainment Weekly*. 'She carried herself like a star.' Dressed in her beloved pink, she was doing her best to cover up her nerves – and had no sense of just what a good job she was doing. She might have felt out of her depth but to Rogers she looked right at home. Then, she and her band mates began to sing. They had chosen the Destiny's Child song 'Emotion'. Rogers was impressed.

As he later recalled, 'The killer was when she opened her mouth to sing. She was a little rough around the edges, but she had this edge to her voice.' In a separate interview with *Kurama* magazine, he described her voice that day as 'raw but distinctive'. He also noticed her burning ambition, saying, 'She wanted this career more than anything.' From the very beginning he believed that she had a chance of having such a career, though he admits that he did not realize just how successful she would become.

After they sang as a three-piece, each of the girls also sang individually. These solo performances only cemented in Rogers' mind that Rihanna was the star. He told her as much and said he wanted to help her get a solo deal. He asked her to return a few days later with her mother so they could discuss his vision. This meant that the days of Contrast were over; Rihanna was about to go it alone. Naturally, this made for an uncomfortable situation with her two band mates. When groups audition they often find that the industry expert will handpick just one member – this sometimes happens on reality television shows like *The X Factor*. It is often awkward: 'It was a really difficult place to be, because obviously I didn't want to hurt my friend's feelings,' Rihanna told *The Observer*. 'I didn't want to betray her, but it was a reality. We had auditioned together and individually, and that was it.' It has never been made clear which of her two friends she was specifically referring to here, though it is believed to be Kelenna, as it was she who craved success the most and therefore took the rejection the hardest.

Suddenly, things were happening quickly. Within forty-eight hours of the audition, Rihanna and her mother were sitting with Rogers as he outlined the early stages of his plan. He would fly the teenager to Connecticut in America so she could record a demo for him to tout around the music industry. Monica found this a prospect that was both exciting and worrisome: would her daughter be safe in the States, and what would happen to her schooling? She realized that, in supporting her daughter's shot at the big time, she would nevertheless have to lay down some rules and boundaries. Rihanna might have resented some of these directives at the time – she was very displeased to be told by Monica that she would have to complete her schooling – but she has since understood that her mother's heart and mind were in just the right place.

She had just under a year of schooling left and, during this time, she took what opportunities she could to polish her performance. She had decided, for instance, to enter her school's annual pageant. She was not a natural fit for such contests: she said she always laughed at them and found them 'stupid'. However, when her school friends dared her to take part, she could not resist taking up the challenge. The pageant fell into several strands. For the beauty strand, Rihanna told the *Daily Mail*, 'My military training came in handy for learning how to balance books on my head for the catwalk.' For the performance contest, she sang the Mariah Carey hit 'Hero'. If one were to be critical, one might say that at times during the performance she over-complicated her rendition with excessive trembling of notes. However, in the context of a singing contest such indulgences are often inevitable. They are also sometimes rewarded, as were hers, with generous audience applause. However, the most striking element of the performance was her confidence. She stood with assurance on the stage, and comfortably added expression to the lyrics with arm and hand movements. During the first break in the vocals she even remembered to smile at the audience. Often, performers her age find such gaps awkward – not Rihanna. She pointed at the audience to tell them they were the heroes of the song, and pointed to the sky when delivering the 'Lord knows' line. Much-needed stage presence was something she had in abundance. To her genuine surprise, she won, and when she was crowned she was bursting with excitement. Ronald, too, was delighted, and proudly told how his daughter had won despite being the youngest participant and a full two years younger than most of those taking part. No wonder she was so thrilled. 'The pageant ended at 11 p.m. and I didn't sleep until, like, 3 a.m.', she told *TMF*.

With success can come the envy of others. Nowadays, Rihanna is all too aware of this. However, when she arrived at school the morning after her pageant victory, she received a rude awakening. 'I lost a lot of people who I thought were my friends. Even the person I thought was my best friend stopped speaking to me,' she told the *Guardian*. The aspect of this that Rihanna found most perplexing was that she saw many of those who were envious as beautiful girls themselves – 'but girls do have insecurities,' she concluded. However, for Rihanna, the future was more important than the present. As well as honing her stage presence and vocal prowess, she also addressed he personal image. The last vestiges of her previous tomboy look were now discarded in favour of an increasingly feminine appearance. 'It was very new and weird for me,' she later told *The Observer*. She went from being a 'barefoot tomboy' to a young lady who 'started getting very fussy with myself' and 'started being very aware'. Her feisty nature survived the cull, though. She would need to draw on it in the exciting times ahead.

*

Such momentum was building around Rihanna's potential in the pop market that Monica's rule that her daughter must finish school before moving to the US was relaxed, and she was allowed to complete her lessons 'on the hop', via private tuition. Suddenly, Rihanna realized, things were getting serious. Leaving the island of her childhood was no great wrench; the glorious weather and stunning scenery had always been overshadowed by her domestic dramas, the widespread prejudices and envies that seemed to be such an unavoidable part of life in such surroundings. While moving to the US was no small change for a girl her age, it was one she was more than prepared to make. 'When I left Barbados, I didn't look back,' she recalled during a chat with *Entertainment Weekly*. 'I wanted to do what I had to do, even if it meant moving to America.'

The day she flew out of Barbados, the island's baking summer was a recent memory, yet as the plane landed in Connecticut, autumn already had the East Coast in its cold grip. Therefore the first steps of her official arrival in the States were huddled ones. Rogers' wife Jackie was waiting to greet her, holding out a metaphorical hand of familiarity. All the same, it was a chilly start to what would be a warm relationship. It was Jackie who took care of the teenager, making sure her laundry was done and ensuring she was fed. 'Jackie definitely took on a mothering role,' admitted Rihanna in an interview with *Giant* magazine. Although she has since credited Jackie with a maternal role, at the time she called her 'auntie'.

For Rihanna, who had sometimes needed to assume a quasi-parental role as a child, it was a blessed relief to be looked after this way, especially during such an unsettling, if exciting, time.

The confidence that Monica had instilled in Rihanna as a child was further tested in this new environment. Although Rogers has said that, from the start, he ensured Rihanna was 'completely involved in all of the business decisions and all that', the lady herself has a different recollection of her status in the early days of her career. 'When I first started, I didn't know anything,' she told the *Guardian*. 'I didn't really have a say.' One central part of her image was the choice of her stage name. With her real first name, Robyn, deemed too commonplace and forgettable for a budding pop star, it was decided that she would need a new name to grab the attention of the industry. 'When I told him my middle name, he preferred that because it was more unique,' she explained to the *Chicago Tribune*. Rihanna it was, and still is. The name is an Arabic word meaning sweet basil.

Meanwhile, her schooling continued. Now, though, she had a private tutor, who could adapt to her student's need for flexibility. As such, Rihanna found herself in a strange position, yet one that is familiar to other popstars who were discovered very young. She was treated as very special by significant figures in the entertainment industry. Yet, just as all this excitement began to go to her head, she was returned to the levelling reality of lessons – suddenly no longer a star, or even a star in the making, but a school pupil. Teenagers are rarely renowned for their patience in the most normal of circumstances. When their heads are being filled with dreams of imminent fame they can find it hard.

So, imagine Rihanna's excitement when she learned she was to audition in front of none other than rap legend Jay-Z. She had been recording a demo CD that could be sent round the labels to showcase her budding talent. It had four tracks on it, including a pair of original compositions: 'Pon de Replay' and 'The Last Time'. The former track leant closely on the sounds of the Caribbean with an almost dancehall reggae feel, while the latter was pure RnB. To spice up the mix she also recorded two cover versions, so prospective labels could hear her voice belt out familiar tunes. Whitney Houston's 'For The Love Of You' and Mariah Carey's trusty classic 'Hero' were both given a Rihanna twist and added to the demo.

Rogers sent the demo to his many contacts in the music industry. As Rihanna told *Interview*, Def Jam Recordings was the first label to respond – and the one to do so with most excitement. 'We got other calls, but they were the most enthusiastic.' She could hardly believe that she was about to audition in front of Jay-Z, a famous and respected musical artist she had known of for many years. Since Jay-Z – real name Shawn Corey Carter – first came to fame in the 1990s he has become a multi-faceted star, respected around the world for his music. 'So I was pretty scared,' she told *Interview* magazine.

The night before the audition she was so anxious she hardly got a wink of sleep. 'I was trying on a million different outfits and make-up,' she told *Glamour*. When she arrived at the label's reception she was already shaking. She had a momentary glimpse of Jay-Z in a hallway. This was the first time she had seen a celebrity of his stature in the flesh.

As she was walked to the audition room, she had a clear mental image of what she would find. Jay-Z, she believed, would be dressed in a suit, and sitting behind a grand desk, smoking a cigar. This rather intimidating image was dispelled when she found that the rapper was, in fact, 'totally chilled, wearing sneakers and a t-shirt'. Alongside the rapper were five bosses from the record company, including the label's boss L.A. Reid, now better known as a judge on *The X Factor USA*, and a man who has long been an enormously influential player in the record business. Despite the more relaxed scene, she still began to shake as she stood there, preparing to sing. Then, like an established artist, her performance mentality kicked in. 'I went into audition mode, I knew it was all or nothing,' she said. She told herself that this bizarre scenario was, in fact, 'an everyday event'. By tricking her own mind that way, she was able to do her best. Again, her impact was quick: Jay-Z has stated he decided to sign her within the first 120 seconds of her audition.

After she had sung, Jay-Z and the record executives took a novel approach to expressing their excitement over what they had just heard: they held her mock-captive. 'They locked me into the office until 3 a.m.,' she recalled during an interview with *The Observer*. Then Jay-Z told her, 'There's only two ways out: out the door after you sign this deal – or through the window.' The office was on the twenty-ninth floor. The scene then turned into one of high drama, as record company executives locked horns with lawyers and other representatives from Rihanna's side. Again, her adolescent impatience kicked in. As her lawyers 'kept talking', she stared at the clock 'waiting to sign'. When the two sides had finished discussing every last clause and syllable of the deal, she signed on the dotted line. Life would never be the same again for the pretty teenager from Barbados. With the Def Jam machinery on her side, she was propelled into a whirlwind of activity. Having for so long wondered when something would happen, suddenly everything seemed to be happening at once.

Within days of signing the deal she was in the studio, heralding a rate of work that even the hugely dedicated

Jay-Z described as at 'an unbelievable breakneck pace'. For Rihanna it was the start of a tough year but one in which she 'grew up so much'. She worked with choreographers for long, exhausting days, sometimes for eight hours at a time. That, though, was just one of her new commitments. 'It taught me the dedication and responsibility it takes to make this dream a reality', she told *Belgrade Net*. She described rising at 5 a.m. and going straight to work on anything from rehearsals, to interviews or video shoots – 'It always seemed glamorous, but it is real work'. After being thrown into the deep end of the industry, her love for music and singing remained, but, she admitted, 'the rose-coloured glasses are no longer so rosy'.

*

Meanwhile, Rihanna's normal life continued as best it could alongside this frenzy. Settling into Connecticut had thrown up regular challenges ever since she shivered her way off the plane on her first day. Indeed, the climate continued to cause a problem. With Rihanna accustomed to the all-year-round warmth of Barbados, she struggled for many months in Connecticut. It was not only the cooler temperatures but also the cycle of seasons that unsettled her. She set out on shopping missions to buy clothes of unfamiliar thickness.

There was also a series of embarrassing incidents involving the young man who cleaned the swimming pool. In the summer, Rihanna liked to recline bare-skinned next to the pool on her days off. It reminded her of being back in Barbados to be able to be so comfortable naked. The only problem was that the pool cleaner kept turning up and surprising her. One imagines he might have enjoyed the view, but for her it was mortifying. But after a while, she told Bravo, the young man became 'used to this view', and in any case she set up a system whereby she would be warned via text message of his impending arrival.

While many of her friends back in Barbados were still living at home with their parents, here she was forging a new life in a strange country. She grew in character enormously during these times, and it was only looking back later that Rihanna fully grasped the effect this move had on her. Already, the trials of her childhood had made her wise beyond her years and stronger emotionally than she might otherwise have had cause to be. 'I've been paying my own bills since I was seventeen, living in a foreign country, and I've always been a little older than my real age,' she later told W magazine.

Rihanna spent three months recording what would be her debut album. 'Pon de Replay' was chosen as her first single. Opening with a drumbeat that is reminiscent of the 1980s UK pop scene, it quickly moves into the festive Caribbean tune that is now so known and loved. The song has a curious name to the outsider: as she explained, the title came from Barbados lingo: 'It's broken English,' she told *Kidz World*. '"Pon" is on, "De" means the, so it's just basically telling the DJ to put my song on the replay.' Ironically, she had been dismissive of the song when it had first been played to her. She felt it sounded like a nursery rhyme rather than a serious pop hit. However, by the time she had finished recording it herself she had changed her view. Putting her own stamp on the track had made her see how good it was. The single, which featured a stunning image of the young lady herself on the sleeve, was released in the US on 24 May 2005. Rihanna was so excited – she had become an officially released recording artist. All the hard work and the many sacrifices had been worth it: she had made it.

Rihanna will never forget the day she first heard the song being played in public. She was at a shopping mall and could hardly believe her ears when it came on the radio. 'I was jumping and screaming, "That's my song"! and everyone was looking at me like I was completely nuts, naturally enough!' It is the sort of moment that every budding popstar dreams of experiencing until it actually happens. For Rihanna it was all part of 'a strange time', in which 'everyone was telling me I was the new

Beyoncé. I was just seventeen and having private tuition to make up for not being at school.'

She awaited the critical response to, and commercial fortune from, the single with both excitement and trepidation. Having lived with her material behind the scenes for what felt like years, it was a curious sensation to suddenly have her music released into the world. The reviews were largely favourable, with scribes casting her as 'a star in the making' with a 'catchy dance tune [that] will get her noticed'. Commercially it did well, particularly for a debut single, reaching the top ten in several countries including the US, UK, Australia and Denmark. Only Mariah Carey's commercial juggernaut of a single 'We Belong Together' kept it off the top spot in the US charts.

'I was in the top ten with huge artists who I looked up to,' Rihanna remembered later in *Glamour* magazine. Those around her, including Jay-Z, did their best to spell out to her what an unusual achievement this was for a debut single. 'This never happens, so don't get used to it,' he told her. What a rollercoaster ride the song had taken her on: from her disappointment and disdain when she first heard its tune to her elation when, having fallen for the song herself, she then watched people around the world also take it to their hearts. Lest she get carried away with the rush of excitement, some of her former classmates in Barbados let it be known they were less impressed with the song, which they argued was a watered-down effort to appeal to mainstream white audiences.

No sooner was her debut single in the shops than last-minute preparations were being made for the release, at the end of August 2005, of her debut album, *Music of the Sun*. As the release date neared, Jay-Z had further important words of counsel for her. He pointed out that there would be harsh and critical reactions to her debut release in some quarters. That much was unavoidable for any artist and for any album. He prepared her for potentially hurtful words and told her the best way to shield herself from them was to just focus on the people who really mattered: her friends and family. She listened closely to what he had to say; after all, he had years of first-hand experience to back up his wisdom.

Ironically, one of the most hurtful things that was said about her at this time concerned her relationship with Jay-Z. The urban news website *Media Takeout* published a 'hatchet job' story, alleging a series of bad characteristics and behaviour on her part. An unnamed former school friend was quoted as saying Rihanna got the deal because she 'forced herself on Jay-Z, because she is extremely promiscuous,' adding, 'Old habits never die.' Rihanna denies any such behaviour, saying, 'That rumour was everywhere.' She described the suggestion as 'disgusting', and added that it made interactions awkward between her and her mentor for a while. She said she would feel 'weird' around him. She believed, accurately, that the source of these rumours was largely a circle of envious people back on the island of her birth. 'It's a silly way of Barbadians,' she said, adding that she fully believed that even many of those who were encouraging to her face were dismissive behind her back.

Starting with the aforementioned 'Pon de Replay', the album was an interesting piece of work. The second track, 'Here I Go Again', a song she was involved in the composition of, is a laidback tune, its understated nature perhaps underlying the universally identifiable theme of the lyrics: a woman resigned to another crack at a compulsive relationship. Track three, 'If It's Lovin' That You Want', is more sassy. Here, she is a temptress, and she plays the part well in a fun, reggae-lite affair.

So far, so safe. Yet the album turns to less predictable terrain when she covers 'You Don't Love Me (No, No, No)'. For a teenager to cover a song associated with the wise, mature voice of Dan Penn was an audacious move. On this track, she invites dancehall reggae star Vybz Kartel to join her and any sense of Rihanna as a play-safe pop puppet is dispatched.

After the dark broodiness of 'You Don't . . .', the mood is lightened by the impish, upbeat 'That La,

La, La'. In the lyrics she taunts other women that their hopes to break her and her man up are doomed to failure, because a love like theirs is hard to find. The chorus has a hint of the nursery rhyme-esque, catchy hook that she would, later in her career, claim as her own. 'The Last Time' is perhaps the album's 'I Will Survive' in terms of theme, though musically it is quite different from the defiant disco classic. Complete with Spanish guitar, it is a mellow soundtrack to a woman emerging from a relationship and vowing that she will never return to it. From a break-up song to a start-up one, 'Willing To Wait' sees her advising a new lover that there is no need to rush matters. One of the album's most mainstream efforts, it is another song of which Rihanna was involved in the writing. Having had her heart broken, the Rihanna in these lyrics is keen to take it slowly as she embarks on a new love. The album's title track was another one she had written, and was also one of the first to be recorded. Plenty of listeners responded to the chorus's encouragement to dance to the music of the sun.

'Let Me' is the album's most upbeat and risqué song. The lyrics are not quite as raunchy as those of future tracks, such as 'S&M', but it is here that this side of her is first heard. 'Rush', which features Kardinal Offishall, maintains the mood, with her singing that she catches a rush whenever she and her boy touch. The electro

'There's a Thug in My Life' sees her cheekily wondering how she will get her 'momma' and her friends to approve of her new man, who has less than pleasant sides to his character. Nobody could have known how her real life would go on to mirror this problem. The slow, mournful ballad 'Now I Know' ends the album. 'Sometimes a happy ending doesn't last,' she sings, completing the record not happily, but powerfully.

The verdicts on the album were mixed. Some critics returned to the comparisons with Beyoncé that were made after her debut single. Ashanti was another artist to whom Rihanna was compared. Among the criticisms levelled at the record were an inconsistency and a too-eclectic mix of styles for the album to form a coherent whole. Some felt it was too long and heavy, particularly for such a young act, while others argued it was too light and frivolous. In later years, Rihanna would take all reviews with a generous pinch of salt – she learned to laugh off the inability of some critics to be pleased with anything. At the time, however, some of the criticisms hurt her.

It is a shame that the harsher words tended to be heard loudest, as among the write-ups for the album were many admiring comments. *The New York Times'* Kelefa Sanneh praised 'There's a Thug in My Life' as a 'pleasant surprise' and a 'cheerfully ridiculous electro-pop ballad'. Its Manhattan tabloid equivalent the *New*

York Post found the album to have 'infectiously catchy' moments. *Rolling Stone* magazine's Barry Walters wrote glowingly of her 'Caribbean charm' and her debut single's 'rhythmic ingenuity'. However, for all this he was unimpressed with the album, rounding on Rihanna as 'a young Mariah Carey minus the birdcalls'. Walters awarded the album two and a half stars out of five. The same score was given by *Slant* magazine, whose reviewer Sal Cinquemani was impressed to find 'the always refreshing touch of pop veterans Evan Rogers and Carl Sturken'. Yet the most positive the reviewer could be in conclusion was to write that 'Rihanna is doing quite well by today's paint-by-numbers RnB standards,' which is faint praise if ever one heard it. *Entertainment Weekly* was harsher, judging the album a 'bland dancehall/ RnB debut' that was 'filled with chintzy production and maudlin arrangements', though at least it praised Rihanna's 'vibrant vocals'. Elsewhere, harsh adjectives such as 'maudlin', 'childish' and 'stale' were employed by reviewers who were, perhaps rightly, disinclined to go easy on her given her debutant status. The *Jamaica Observer* said the album took listeners on an 'enjoyable ride', its reviewer purring that she 'proves that music can, and does, cover all your emotions and you can sing about the good times and the bad times.' A rather pedestrian observation, but a welcome one. The *Daily Telegraph* praised her 'arresting voice'.

As would always be the case, it was the commercial performance that was the most significant factor. The album reached the top ten of the US Billboard charts, another surprising success for a debut release. Rihanna and her team were very proud of this achievement. Overseas it fared less well: it climbed no higher than number thirty-five in the UK charts and only made number ninety-three in France. It was unable to mirror the fast-track success of her debut single in other territories, though in time it did notch up an impressive number of sales.

Many of those sales came as a result of the live performances she delivered in the months after the album's release. Rihanna's management had, shrewdly, already given her some early experience of large live audiences while she was still working on her debut releases. She had been offered support slots with 50 Cent in Canada and Gwen Stefani in Japan. She was learning from more and more famous mentors, so, even before she embarked on her live dates in the wake of the album's release, she was already well rehearsed in all aspects of large-scale live performance.

Her debut tour was backed by a commercial tie-in with a cosmetics company and was entitled 'Rihanna's Secret Body Spray Tour'. For these dates the venues were smaller than those in which she had performed during her previous support slots, but she was arriving at them as the headline act. The audience created a noisy, electric and exciting atmosphere and the tracks performed included cover versions and mash-ups of other artists' songs, as well as the key tracks from her album. With the dates finished, she flew back to Barbados for Christmas. While she was pleased to catch up with those whom she loved and cared for, the visit home again reminded her of the petty nature of some Barbadians. All too aware of some of the icy remarks that had been made about her, she told herself that it was a good thing to have escaped such an environment.

*

Rihanna returned to the island in January for the most triumphant of reasons, yet her difficult relationship with Barbados continued. She made the trip to attend the inaugural Barbados Music Awards ceremony. She had been nominated in ten categories, so she was very excited as she arrived at the Sherbourne Centre in Bridgetown. She won in eight of the ten categories, which included female artist of the year, entertainer of the year and best new artist. While accepting the awards, she thanked the people of the island for their support.

Having recently struck a commercial deal to promote Barbados as a tourist destination, in the eyes of many she had become the de facto face of the island.

Speaking about her new promotional role, she was thrilled to be involved with the campaign, and credited Barbados as 'the country which made me who I am'. Elsewhere she beamed that the people of Barbados were 'really supporting me', and said how 'grateful' she was to them. Yet, behind these positive statements was the bitter truth that some of her fellow islanders were slandering her. Privately, she raged that it 'physically hurt' some Barbadians to offer compliments to or be pleased for those who enjoyed success. She added that they 'talk shit about me all the time', despite the fact that she was working so hard to 'put them on the map'. She felt these efforts were taken for granted by people who found it 'easier to be mean'. While she understood the need to 'smile for the cameras' when it came to comments about Barbados, her feisty nature and inherent sense of justice made it hard for her to resist the temptation to speak out against those who whispered so sourly against her.

In time, her inner anger subsided to an extent as she realized that the greatest way to answer one's critics is to live well. When she was nominated for a gong at the 2005 MTV Europe Music Awards, she was given a hint of the huge things to come. So she worked hard on her career, quickly releasing her second album, *A Girl Like Me*. As its title suggests, this was an album of increased confidence, sassiness and personal poise.

Released in the spring of 2006, it followed hot on the heels of her debut. She had started recording it even as her first album was just reaching the stores. 'We just had to fit it in where we could, like at the end of the day,' she said of the recording process. 'Like, at 11.30 at night, we would start . . . we had no time.' With such coordinated activity centred on her it was clear that her label and management had little doubt about her ability. As for Rihanna, she basked in this speedy progression to album two. 'That's what's great about the music business,' she told ARTISTdirect. ' When you feel it's time, you just go for it . . . we pretty much dived right in.'

And what of the resultant splash? Rihanna felt that vocally she had 'matured so much', and that lyrically she now had particular confidence. 'Now I'm singing about experiences that I've gone through and stuff that other eighteen-year-old girls go through, so it's all about progression,' she told MTV. Impressive progression at that. The stand-out track of *A Girl Like Me* was its lead single, 'S.O.S.'. With its sample riff taken from the 1980s UK pop classic 'Tainted Love' by Soft Cell, it is an infectiously catchy piece of pop. The lyrics concern a toxic relationship that she needs to be rescued from. 'I call out for help,' she explained, to be saved from a 'crazy feeling that this guy gives me'. In the story of Rihanna's musical development, this song constitutes a significant moment. It was a game-changer for sure, a song fairly described by one newspaper as 'a fine bid for world domination'. The next single from the album was 'Unfaithful', a track that cast the female as the villain in a relationship. In it, she mourns her own tendency to infidelity, while reinforcing her refusal to be a victim. The album's title track, for which Rihanna is credited as co-writer, was fresh terrain for the starlet at this stage of her career. Later converts will not be surprised by its smooth soulfulness. Yet at the time it was a new sound and vibe. Though it has elements of RnB, it is the sort of tune that any mainstream, crossover soul singer would relish. In 'Kisses Don't Lie', another track she is credited with co-writing, the music is a straightforward blend of rock and reggae but on this track in particular she sounds so much better than she had anywhere on her debut album. In 'We Ride', the roles of 'Unfaithful' are reversed: here it is her who has been cheated on. However, as she told MTV, she was not one to dwell on such disappointment. 'If you want to do that, and be ugly and unfaithful, then I can just do my thing, chill with my girls and have fun,' she said.

Having promised that the album would be true to herself, in 'Dem Haters' Rihanna tackled the Barbadian 'haters' who had targeted her with gossip and harsh criticisms as her success and fame had built. With the chorus about people smiling to your face and then turning their wrath on you when your back is turned, this song well and truly captured her feelings. 'Final Goodbye' is a beautiful tear-jerker, and a fitting successor to the defiance of 'Dem Haters'. It builds beautifully and reveals yet more depth to her repertoire. 'A Million Miles Away', complete with gorgeously rich piano, is of a similar ilk. In 'Break It Off', Rihanna returns to the more modern reggae style of *Music of the Sun*. Sean Paul's presence on the track means she could hardly have avoided the dancehall style. Were this the only song of hers one had heard, the listener would never believe she could have also covered other genres such as rock, ballad, disco and pop. However, it is towards the more traditional reggae style of Bob Marley that she leans in 'Crazy Little Thing Called Love'. 'Selfish Girl', too, is reggae-lite; it is also inoffensive to the point of being forgettable. In 'P.S. (I'm Still Not Over You)', however, Rihanna is trying to erase from her own memory the traces of a broken relationship. Her second album ends with the puckish 'If It's Lovin' That You Want (Part 2)'.

The critics dug deeper in their subsequent analysis, as they now had two albums to compare and contrast. *Vibe* magazine used words such as 'coquettish' and 'charisma' before concluding that 'some things are better the second time around.' *USA Today* declared Rihanna to be 'at ease riding a groove', and said the album was 'bubbling' and contained 'depth'. *Rolling Stone* had its issues, not least with the record's non-single 'filler' tracks, but overall felt it was 'much more likeable'. *The New York Times* was scathing, judging it to be a 'scattershot album [. . .] full of duds'. MTV announced that Rihanna was 'getting in touch with her rock side'.

These articles contained mixed messages and varying degrees of approval but their true relevance at this stage of the story is their very existence: column inches about Rihanna that focused on her music. In the years to come, she would become such a large-scale global celebrity that the majority of printed words about her would entirely ignore her musical output in favour of focusing on her personal life. As her life became increasingly stormy, it also became ever more fascinating.

3.

A Star is Born

With non-stop releases throughout 2005 and 2006, Rihanna had been keeping the charts and the stores busy. In the space of just fourteen months she had put out two albums and five singles. Yet, despite this, little was known and understood about the woman behind the music. Due to recurring comparisons between her and Beyoncé Knowles the public's knowledge of Rihanna's music was not being mirrored by its understanding of her as a human being. She was now enjoying commercial success in several territories, yet sustained careers are rarely built by anonymous artists: she needed to spend less time in the studio and more time out in the public eye.

As part of this quest, she let it be known she would be receptive to non-musical gigs. For instance, she took on her first acting role, starring in a high-school film entitled *Bring It On: All Or Nothing*, in which she played the organizer of a cheerleading competition. This was a straight-to-DVD movie and there was nothing overly artistic about it, nor anything particularly demanding about her role. Later, she remarked to *Interview* magazine that she was 'basically being myself' in the film, adding: 'I never really had to act.' So she had merely dipped her toe in the pool, yet the experience had thrilled and inspired her; she told her team that she would definitely like more acting work in the future.

*

As Rihanna showed more of herself to the world, speculation grew over her personal life. Which man was this stunning new star stepping out with, the media wondered. They reported, with varying accuracy, on connections between her and numerous men. Around this time, she did date the actor Shia LaBeouf – but only once. It was Rihanna who made the first move, sending him a text as he filmed a movie. 'It never got beyond one date,' the *Transformers* star ruefully revealed to *Playboy* magazine. 'The spark wasn't there.' Another actor she was linked to was Josh Hartnett, the star of a raft of successful films including *The Virgin Suicides* and *40 Days and 40 Nights*. Some reports excitedly suggested the two were in a full-on relationship; however, she would later clarify during an interview with *Allure* magazine that the media had overestimated the extent of their interaction. 'He and my management, they have each other's contact information,' she began. 'I went to Pink Elephant, and he came by. All of a sudden, the next day I'm seeing that we were kissing and hugging each other. You can't even go out with a friend who's a celebrity and have a good time without people making shit up.' Focusing on the positives, she smiled as she added: 'Well, at least he's good-looking, right?'

At this stage, her romantic life was actually on a back

burner. A difficult relationship with a 'very insecure boyfriend' meant she was happy to fly solo for a while. As she explained to *Sugar* magazine, 'He kept breaking up with me for no reason, I'd cry all night and he'd just assume we would get back together the next day.' For a while, she felt stuck in this cycle, but she eventually summoned the strength to draw a line and cut him out of her life. Though it 'took ages to get over him', she did so eventually, not least thanks to her friends. She also offered a manifesto for her approach to love, saying that men who 'move too fast' are showing a lady that they do not see her as 'special'. Any man, she said, who 'tried to get frisky with me when we don't even know each other' would be swiftly dispatched. Tragically, she would in due course be embroiled in a relationship that caused many to fear for her safety.

*

In the meantime her working life continued apace. She founded a charity, entitled the Believe Foundation. According to the Foundation's website, it 'gives children a chance by providing everything from medical attention for children who can't afford it, school supplies for children in poorly funded public schools, toys for children who are terminally ill and clothes for children in homeless shelters'. Her motivation for doing so, Rihanna explained, had begun long before she was famous. 'When I was young and I would watch television and I would see all the children suffering, I always said when I grow up I want to help,' she said at a Believe event. 'Not long after I was in the position where I could help. I started to visit all these children's hospitals and I have a soft spot for kids,' she continued. 'I just want to help and make sure they are happy.' When stars form charities or foundations their efforts are often greeted sceptically and many are suspicious that they are fuelled as much by vanity as they are philanthropy. But in grounding the genesis of her motivation in the time before she was famous Rihanna managed to avoid such criticisms.

She also signed up to a fashion project aimed at helping the fight against AIDS. Fashion Against AIDS saw Rihanna team up with Good Charlotte and Timbaland, alongside Scissor Sisters, Ziggy Marley, My Chemical Romance, Tiga and Rufus Wainwright, to work with the respected fashion designers Henrik Vibskov and Katharine Hamnett. They produced a range of clothes, including t-shirts and tank tops, to raise both awareness and funds for AIDS charities.

Of particular concern to Rihanna was the fact that fifty per cent of those newly infected with HIV were aged between fifteen and twenty-four. 'I love fashion and I love that it can be used in such a positive way to fight

AIDS,' she said. 'I wanted to get involved with Fashion Against AIDS because it's a scary disease and it affects a lot of young people out there.'

She also lent her vocals to a single called 'Just Stand Up', which benefited the Stand Up to Cancer campaign. The single featured a galaxy of stars including Mariah Carey, Beyoncé, Fergie, Miley Cyrus and Leona Lewis. Rihanna had finally earned her place alongside such big names.

Rihanna has continued to help source bone marrow donors with donor center DKMS and, in a separate project, she also spearheaded a drive to find a donor for a desperate leukemia-stricken mother of two from New York. When she first heard of the plight of Lisa Gershowitz-Flynn, who was suffering from an aggressive form of cancer called acute myelogenous leukemia, Rihanna made a public plea for a bone marrow donor to come forward. Her high-profile appeal worked, and Rihanna expressed her joy at the news that a donor had been found. 'There are no words to express how happy I am for Lisa and her family,' she told *People*. 'I am so thankful she found a donor and I feel honoured to be a part of such an amazing miracle.'

Her delight for Lisa's children also struck on a central theme of her overall charitable effort: to protect children from the sort of hurt that blighted her own developing years. 'I just want to travel all over the world with the kids,' she said. 'As a kid, the thing I hated most was disappointment, so I never want to disappoint kids. I always want to put a smile on their faces. Kids are the future.' Likewise, it became increasingly clear, charitable work would be a large part of her own future.

Ultimately, though, of course, it was music that was and is the focus of Rihanna's career. The challenge facing her and her team was to determine how her image could be best managed in order to bring that music to as wide a number of people as possible. Her fame was already considerable, yet she yearned to approach the stature of the truly big names of the music industry. Becoming the 'black Madonna' was a long-held and smouldering ambition of the Barbadian.

So it was time for a new regime. She valued the care that had been taken over her career in its early days – but only to an extent. With the extra confidence that her media presence gave her, she now wanted something different. 'I reinvented myself,' she said, looking back later. Pertinently, she decided that 'having fun' was more important than 'being careful'. After all, she reasoned playfully, 'bad girls take risks' – a theme that would surround her activity for the foreseeable future.

Indeed, that theme embraced both the title and essence of her next album – and she had an exciting music figure on board for the production team: the American rapper, producer and actor Ne-Yo. As she worked with Ne-Yo in the studio, he offered her more than just production notes. For the first time in her career, she got vocal training in the studio itself. 'He is such a genius,' smiled Rihanna. 'He'll tell me how to breathe and stuff.' On one occasion, he asked her to sing in a more staccato style. A baffled Rihanna replied: 'OK, I don't know what that is!' She needed to learn more about the nuts and bolts of music in order to construct ever-improving products. Furthermore, every bit of knowledge she acquired added to her poise and confidence. She was a willing pupil.

So, having ploughed a fairly steady and consistent professional path until now, Rihanna was itching for a thrilling diversion. She took such a turn with the new album; she described *Good Girl Gone Bad* as 'a big turning point'. Her mentor Jay-Z sang from the same hymn sheet – and with admiration in his tone. 'She's found her voice,' he said. 'That's the best thing for any label, to have an artist step in and take control of their own career – she's left the nest.'

Speaking to the *Star Phoenix*, Rihanna outlined how her image and approach had changed. 'I basically took the attitude of the bad girl and I really got rebellious and just did everything the way I wanted to do it – I didn't want to listen to anybody, I didn't consult with anybody.' She added: 'I just reinvented myself.' Her reinvention was all-encompassing. She wanted to differentiate herself from her previous image as a young artist who did what she was told. Having stated during a promotional interview for *A Girl Like Me* that she didn't like to be 'too much in control' of the choice of songs and that she would 'get advice from producers', she had uncomfortable perceptions to shrug off. Her look changed, too. Fresh tattoos were painted on her body, her hair was cut shorter and her outfits became more sexy.

Her promotional videos would also take a raunchier turn, as we shall see. As Jon Bream of the *Star Tribune* commented, Rihanna's videos are central to her appeal as an artist. 'In the tradition of Madonna and Janet Jackson, Rihanna has become the video vixen of the '00s . . . [she] has perfected the pout, the long-legged strut and trend-setting hairdos that keep women and men alike checking her out on YouTube,' he said.

But Rihanna was keen to distinguish between raunchy and sleazy. Indeed, during a radio interview, referring to the album title and her overall image shift, she said: 'Bad is not sleazy.' Instead, she explained, she had in mind a 'bad' more in keeping with that of the 1980s Michael Jackson album of the same name. In terms of image, then, she was succeeding in ringing the changes. She admitted in an interview with *The Observer* that at first she had merely accepted 'what was given to me', but she had since begun to become more critical.

'I said, "I don't want to wear that and I want to wear my hair like this." Now I'm in complete control of my image and everything else. It takes time. You learn.'

These cosmetic changes, though, did not address the suspicions that had plagued her since she first became famous: that the extent of her creative input into her actual material had always been minimal. Far from stepping up the level of her input for album three, she actually took less of a song-writing role. Speaking to *Entertainment Weekly*, she was unabashed about this, explaining that if a song that was brought to her was 'great' as it stood, she was disinclined to mess with it just for the sake of getting a 'publishing credit' (her name listed alongside the songwriters). 'It's not about that,' she said. 'It's about making great music.'

This was fine logic in as far as it went. The point that rather hung in the air for several critics was that a true artist would insist on being at the heart of the creative process. This was about more than musical 'credibility' – an essentially nebulous concept at the best of times. Instead, listeners wanted to understand the woman behind the music. The soaring emotional punch of singers such as Amy Winehouse and Adele has been that their songs of heartbreak and tragedy were true and had happened to them personally. In this confessional age of social networking, it is artists who are similarly confessional who pack the hardest punch. Without this dimension to their music success will be hard earned.

Hard earned but not impossible – as Rihanna was about to prove. The fact that she had no hand in the composition of her third album's songs did not prevent it from becoming a commercial sensation. Its success was due, in large part, to the presence of one particular track. It is, on its single version, four minutes and fourteen seconds long with a 'West Indian groove' that would change forever the life of a girl from Barbados. But she very nearly did not get to record the song. She had to fight for it, and the fact that she did so with such determination suggests she realized its potential right away. 'It was so crazy,' she told Craig McLean of the *Daily Telegraph*, 'because that particular record, it was a battle to get it.' The song's name? 'Umbrella'.

The story of 'Umbrella' begins in 2003, when composer Tricky Stewart was working with Britney Spears on her album *In The Zone*. He enjoyed the experience, so when, nearly four years later, he, along with other members of his team The-Dream and Kuk Harrell, felt he had a potentially massive hit track on his hands, it was Spears's camp he was in touch with first. Unfortunately for Spears, life was tough in 2007. She was going through testing times emotionally, with her career perilously close to disaster. Therefore, the song rather passed her and her team by.

'Her current state was a little bizarre, you know?'

Stewart later told *MTV News*. 'It wasn't meant to be.' So he decided to look elsewhere for a home for the song. There was talk of it being handed to a new girl group, or even earmarked for the RnB singers Akon or Taio Cruz. However, Stewart actually sent it to two parties: the representatives of soul diva Mary J. Blige, and L.A. Reid, of Rihanna's label Def Jam. Over the next ten days, both parties would express fierce interest in the track, launching The-Dream and Stewart into 'the bidding war of our lives', as the latter recalled.

Blige, a mammoth star at the peak of her powers with eight nominations to her name at the imminent GRAMMY Awards ceremony, was their clear first choice. Even Rihanna was under no illusions as to why Blige would be a more tempting act for a songwriter with a potential gem: 'Any songwriter would die for her to sing one of their songs,' she told the *Daily Telegraph*.

Yet, in part due to her enormous investment in the forthcoming GRAMMYs, Blige was proving difficult to track down for a decision. The composers were happy to wait. 'At the time, if you heard Mary's name and you heard Rihanna's name, you'd want to hold out [for Blige's response],' Stewart said. 'Mary's coming off "Be Without You"; she's nominated for all these GRAMMYs, the whole thing. So the plan with us, really, was to hold the record to get a response from Mary.'

The GRAMMYs proved to be a godsend for

Rihanna's effort to secure the rights to 'Umbrella'. Not only did the preparations for the ceremony delay Blige's decision, but on the night itself it allowed Rihanna to approach one of the songwriters and stake a solid claim to the song. 'I went up to him: "Listen, 'Umbrella' is my song,"' she recalled. 'He must have thought I was really pushy and laughed it off. But I held his face and I turned it back to my own: "No, I'm serious: I need 'Umbrella'."'

Fuelling her boldness was a basic sense of justice: how could the songwriters have dangled such a song in front of her if they were also offering it to someone else? It was a determined pitch and it did the trick: within forty-eight hours she was handed the song. Regular phonecalls to the writers from L.A. Reid's office – as regularly as every twenty minutes for an entire weekend, according to one account – had helped tip things her way. Yet the simple fact was clear: Rihanna's boldness had played a key role in their decision. The girl cast as a pliable puppet had shown she could seize control of her destiny – and what a destiny 'Umbrella' would create.

A few days after she landed the song, hip-hop royalty Jay-Z agreed to contribute a rapped introduction. He said that the minute he first heard it he knew it would be a 'smash'. As he considered Rihanna and her team to be 'family', it was an easy decision for him to come on board. Rihanna got goosebumps when she first heard his contribution. She could hardly believe her luck; life felt good.

For her and her team the song had the potential to be not just a huge hit, but a groundbreaking and career-defining one. Its catchy hook of 'ella, ella, eh, eh, eh' was already superb on the guide track presented to Rihanna. By the time she put her own unique twist on it, it was nothing short of iconic. Therefore, for the promotional video, Rihanna had insisted she wanted to create something 'extraordinary', and 'really, really out there'. The song itself was enough to capture the imagination; she wanted the video to throw away the key. The production team took on board her wishes and created a fine video. In it, by the time the second verse begins, she has already been featured in three outfits. Prancing on her tiptoes in several scenes, gazing at the camera provocatively, and pulling shapes to emphasize her physique – she had never looked so sexy.

All that before the scene featuring her 'wearing' just silver spray paint. She told *Men's Fitness* magazine that the bodypaint look was one she would 'only do once in my lifetime'. Two women applied the spray, and it was done so thoroughly that Rihanna was covered in several coats. The scene itself was shot in a separate box, so only a limited number of people – around eight, including the star herself – could see her effectively naked. One of the assistants involved with the shoot actually burst into tears as they were filming it, so moved was she by the power of what they were producing.

By the end of the video, as Rihanna beckons the viewer to 'come into me', she had won the hour. The filming had been an intense experience for all concerned – it took Rihanna several days to remove all traces of the silver spray paint from her body – but the result had been well worth it. Between the video and the song, Team Rihanna believed they had the tools to conquer the world's charts.

All this excitement was justified. *AllMusic* could hardly contain its excitement over the song's 'mammoth if spacious drums' and 'towering backdrop during the chorus'. However, it was the partial disinterest of Rihanna's vocal delivery – 'an ideal spot between trying too hard and boredom, like she might've been on her twentieth take' – that had most piqued the critic's interest. In contrast, the *Guardian* loved the single's ardour, describing it as an 'impassioned declaration of us-against-the-world devotion'. Over in the US, there was more acclaim. *The New York Times* put it best, describing 'Umbrella' as 'a space-age hip-hop song'.

As for the public, they could just not stop singing along. Commercially, the song became a juggernaut of success that accelerated straight to the number-one spot in several countries across the world, including

Australia, the USA and the UK, where it hit the top on
digital sales alone and stayed there for ten consecutive
weeks, giving Rihanna her first UK number-one single.
Indeed, the demand for digital downloads was so huge
that at one point iTunes crashed under the pressure.
This made for great PR, thus creating yet more demand
for the song and forming a profitable, albeit vicious,
circle. Other countries in which 'Umbrella' hit the top
spot included Ireland, Germany, France, Sweden and
Canada.

After the reviews and the sales came the accolades.
Entertainment Weekly put the song at the summit of its
top-ten singles of 2007, while *Time* and *Rolling Stone*
magazines included it in the top three of their respective
top-100 singles of the year. When it came to awards
ceremonies, it also fared with rude health, winning a
brace of gongs at the MTV Video Awards ceremony and
also two *Billboard* honours.

At the GRAMMYs, the song was nominated in three
categories: Song of the Year, Record of the Year and Best
Rap/Sung Collaboration. There was a nice serendipity to
this: the previous year's GRAMMYs ceremony had played
an important role in Rihanna's successful snatching of
the song from the potential grasp of Mary J. Blige; now
here she was herself at the 2007 ceremony on the cusp
of winning three awards for it. On the night itself, she
was victorious only in the Best Rap/Sung category –

upon accepting the award she gave a shout-out to her birthplace, saying: 'Barbados – we got one!' – yet by then the song had brought her critical and commercial rewards that matched her hopes. 'Umbrella' was also listed as the United World Chart top song of the year. It topped the charts in over forty countries.

However, the impact of the single went way beyond awards. Thanks in the main to its infectious refrain of 'ella, ella, eh, eh, eh . . .' it captured the imagination of a considerable chunk of the planet's pop fans throughout the spring and into the summer. It also earned Rihanna a commercial endorsement deal with an umbrella manufacturer, as she explained during an interview with Q magazine. 'I did have a deal with an umbrella company and they had a range of very good umbrellas,' she said. 'This is kind of weird because I grew up in Barbados and there's not a great culture of umbrellas like there is in the UK and Europe. I guess we have the occasional storm or maybe the Caribbean is more known for its hurricanes and an umbrella isn't going to get you very far in a situation like that. But, yes, I have a few umbrellas. Maybe ten? I dunno, but I am very grateful to the umbrella for what it has done for my career.' (Since becoming famous Rihanna has not been short of endorsement deals. Before she turned twenty-two she had already signed commercial agreements with Nike, Clinique, Happy, UNICEF and Gucci, Totes

Umbrellas, and Secret Body Spray.)

In the UK, the release of 'Umbrella 'coincided with a downpour of rain. Prior to the release, Britain had been basking in unseasonably warm and dry conditions, but twenty-four hours after the single hit the shops those pleasant temperatures were a thing of the past. Britain was in for one of the wettest summers in living memory. As the rain continued to pour, flooding struck several regions and the summer turned into a washout. Meanwhile, Rihanna's voice, offering listeners the chance to stand under her 'um-ber-ella' seemed as ubiquitous as the rain itself.

This proved to be a blessing and a curse when it came to publicity for the song. UK tabloids, desperate to tell the British public what it already knew – that it was actually raining an awful lot – made connections between the song and the wetness. *The Sun*, for instance, wondered if Rihanna had cursed the country. It launched a tongue-in-cheek campaign for readers to 'flush' the song 'down the drain' where, the paper quipped, 'it brolly well belongs'.

In reality, all these reports merely attracted more attention to the song, and were therefore grist to the mill. As for Rihanna herself, she admitted that some Brits had been 'grilling' her about her potential part in the rainy summer. She assured them that it was nothing more than a coincidence. In fact, she concluded, rather than her song keeping Britain wet, it was Britain's wetness that was keeping her song at the top of the charts. Along the way, she hoped, 'Umbrella' would at least be offering an upbeat dimension to the grim conditions. 'People hate the rain, but here was this song that speaks about the rain and makes you feel great – even if the weather is horrible,' she told Q magazine.

The song continued to generate commercial deals. The men's grooming brand Gillette awarded Rihanna with 'Celebrity Legs of a Goddess'. As part of the publicity gimmick, they insured her legs for a cool $1million. This sparked subsequent rumours that she had insured other parts of her anatomy. She also had a deal with the Covergirl cosmetics range. How could she reconcile such a mainstream and demure commercial brand with her aim to be more edgy? She argued that her Covergirl moments gave her the chance to take a break from the 'hardcore' and 'anti-innocent' drive and keep 'in touch with my feminine side'. She was enjoying it; as she told digital magazine Concrete Loop: 'I feel fun again, and it's fun playing around with the make-up.'

*

With her star shining ever brighter, the songstress saw numerous requests for collaborations with other artists. Many of those who requested to work with her were politely declined, but one offer that she did take up came from American rapper T.I., when she agreed to lend her vocals to his song 'Live Your Life'. The track was featured on his album, *Paper Trail*, and released as a single in its own right. It sold well, reaching the top five in several countries, and Rihanna's involvement in it earned it a gong at the People's Choice Awards on 6 January 2010, where it triumphed in the Favourite Music Collaboration category. She also signed up for a collaboration with Pussycat Doll Nicole Scherzinger, alongside whom she recorded a song called 'Winning Women' for a deodorant company.

And so the determination Rihanna showed in securing 'Umbrella' was paying off. Critically, commercially, influentially, and in terms of overall public cultural consciousness, it had proved to be *the* song of 2007. A chart-topper worldwide, it sold over 6 million copies and smashed a number of records. Its journey to the UK top spot on the strength of digital downloads alone was a first for a female artist, for instance. She loved setting this record. 'So I made history there and it astounded me, being number one,' she told *Concrete Loop*. 'Then I came back here and got an email saying that "Umbrella" just became number one on the *Billboard* 100 chart. Making history and just making that impression – like, that makes me think this will be my biggest album with this big single. This new me and this new project is definitely going to be the highlight of my career, and it's something that I know I will never forget for as long as I am doing this.'

The song was widely covered, including by unlikely artists such as Manic Street Preachers, and My Chemical Romance. So many people wanted to claim their slice of reflected glory. It put our heroine firmly on the map and whetted the public's appetite for the album to follow.

The album *Good Girl Gone Bad* opens with the single's A-side. Therefore, the first vocal heard is that of Jay-Z. For a song that has become one of the twenty-first century's biggest hits, 'Umbrella' is a track with surprisingly laid-back vocals. Compared with, say, 'Don't Stop The Music', Rihanna sounds almost lethargic – deliberately, of course. One fascinating dimension of the song is how Rihanna's vocal delivery somehow lifts entirely gentle, innocent lyrics into something more edgy. On paper, the chorus has a nursery rhyme-like quality, but by the time Rihanna's finished with it, it sounds far more adult. No wonder *Time* magazine declared it 'the sexiest song of 2007'.

Then, 'Shut Up And Drive' takes the album into feistier, up-tempo terrain. A perfect summertime track, its feeling is entirely light and carefree. 'Hate That I Love You' takes the album in a gentler, acoustic direction; this breezy duet with Ne-Yo is as close to folk as Rihanna is likely to get. A number of critics have compared it with Beyoncé's 'Irreplaceable'. As the third track's soft acoustic sounds fade out, the listener is scarcely ready for the attention-grabbing opening to its successor, 'Don't Stop The Music'. Rihanna's opening plea is joined by the track's fierce techno beats. The bass drum dominates this multi-layered, urgently delivered song. From early on, the 'Mama-say, mama-sa, ma-ma-ko-ssa' chant from Michael Jackson's disco hit 'Wanna Be Startin' Somethin'' can be heard in the background. An exuberant and demanding song, it is perfect for club dance floors. Rarely has she sounded as sexy. 'Push Up On Me', in which she sings the praises of assured men, is similarly sassy. Then *Good Girl Gone Bad* takes another diversion, this time into ballad territory in the shape of 'Take A Bow'. Downbeat and gentle, it is a sad and weary song. Like 'Hate That I Love You', it has also attracted comparisons with 'Irreplaceable' – in this case for its lyrics more than its sound. Accused of being 'lifeless' and underwhelming by the critics, it also saw Rihanna accused of sounding 'bored'. While in 'Umbrella' her detached vocals were deliberate and effective, in 'Take A Bow' the effect is less positive. To many listeners, though, this was the perfect soundtrack for the moment of resignation at the end of a flawed relationship. 'But it's over now,' she sang, infusing the words with just the right flavour of regret. Then there is the racier 'Rehab', a song title borrowed from singer Amy Winehouse.

This sparked a seemingly furious posting on Twitter by Winehouse, who wrote: 'Rihanna, you owe me!' (Given the late Miss Winehouse's rough sense of humour, it is likely that she was joking, and that the Twitter battle was merely a mutually beneficial publicity stunt.)

With so many genres crammed into one album, *Good Girl Gone Bad* constituted a palpably bold release from Rihanna. It fitted her mood of the moment, which required a change in direction, but how would such a departure be received? the *Guardian* felt she was 'ill-suited' to the dancier, poppier tracks, and missed the 'summery reggae' of her previous albums. The paper's reviewer, Alex Macpherson, described the album overall as a 'curate's egg' – by which he meant good in parts. *Slant* magazine's reviewer also expressed mixed feelings, concluding: '*Good Girl Gone Bad* is far from a great album, but it guarantees Rihanna, who's unequivocally a singles artist, at least a few more shiny hits to tuck under her belt.' *Rolling Stone* saw the whole thing more positively, awarding it four and a half stars out of five. *AllMusic*, meanwhile, entirely removed its hat to the album. 'From beginning to end, *Good Girl Gone Bad* is as pop as pop gets in 2007, each one of its twelve songs a potential hit in some territory,' raved Andy Kellman. The BBC website was also positive, ruling: 'If being bad does this for Rihanna, then being good is, like, totally overrated'; its reviewer also suggested that other tracks on the album were even 'better' than the ever-popular 'Umbrella'. *Entertainment Weekly* said: 'At its finest, messiest moments, *Good Girl Gone Bad* is a thrilling throwback to more than a decade ago,' when RnB and hip-hop were merged to 'create chunky jeep anthems'.

The verdicts of the critics may have been mixed, but the commercial performance of the album was very healthy. It netted Rihanna her first UK album chart number one – also hitting the top spot in Canada and Ireland – and reached as high as number two in the US. With the album flying, more singles followed: 'Shut Up And Drive', 'Hate That I Love You', 'Take A Bow', 'Disturbia' and 'If I Never See Your Face Again' were released in their own right. 'Shut Up And Drive' became her fifth number-five single in the UK, while 'Hate That ...' reached only number fifteen. However, the next two singles truly lived up to the glory of 'Umbrella', with 'Take A Bow' hitting the summit of the charts in several countries including the US, the UK, Ireland and Sweden, and 'Disturbia' becoming a top-ten hit in a handful of territories.

In 2009, Rihanna released a remix version of the album entitled, appropriately, *Good Girl Gone Bad: The Remixes*. Featuring energetic, club-style reworkings of the album's tracks by Moto Blanco, Tony Moran, Soul Seekerz and Wideboys, it received a mixed reception from the critics and its commercial success was modest by Rihanna's already high standards. Yet it helped give the album yet more life ahead of the next conventional release. With three albums in as many years, she laughed off the observation that she was releasing at a speedy rate. Yet she understood why it was a talking point.

*

As Rihanna's star rose, her live performances also became, on occasion, increasingly astounding affairs. In the wake of impressive album sales, she undertook her most ambitious tour to date, playing eighty dates in thirty countries over a six-month period. She had a lot to prove as she set out on the road afresh, as her previous efforts had been truly damned in some quarters. For instance, after a concert at the Ottawa Bluesfest in 2006, she had earned a devastating review from *Jam! Showbiz* scribe Denis Armstrong. He wrote: 'The music took a backseat to fashion as Rihanna had a hard time singing in tune, while her dancing was little more than strutting back and forth. Meanwhile, her hyperactive DJ kept telling us to make some noise, which I thought Rihanna was already doing sufficiently well on her own throughout a dreary and embarrassingly short forty-minute set.' On the *Good Girl Gone Bad* tour, she hit back strongly with some improved performances. These were energetic and grand, and she was backed by a six-strong band and a quartet of dancers. She typically launched her set with 'Pon De Replay', before diving into more recent and familiar material. She also covered Bob Marley's classic reggae song 'Is This Love'. One reviewer described one of her outfits as 'a sexy, dominatrix-like studded black leather ensemble'. Another said that she looked as if she had just stepped out of a sex shop. Fittingly, Rihanna would close the set with her most popular song, 'Umbrella', a perfect climax that was lapped up by audiences.

Along the way, an MTV reviewer described the concert as 'not the most mind-blowing' she had seen, and another reviewer complained of 'tuneless mangling' and compared Rihanna's dancing – unfavourably – to that of a one-legged woman. Negatives used in reviews included 'mechanical', 'robotic', 'un-erotic' and 'cold'. But the moments in which Rihanna managed to unite venues into dancing along, particularly to 'Don't Stop The Music', were magisterial. By the time the tour climaxed in Mexico, she had learned many lessons and honed her skills. Future tours would be far more polished and convincing affairs.

She also embarked on the 'Glow in the Dark Tour' with Kanye West, Lupe Fiasco, and N.E.R.D. During this period, she also made appearances on television shows and at industry ceremonies. For example, in September 2008 she flew to Las Vegas to perform at the MTV Video

Music Awards. She sang a mash-up of pop classics, including the Michael Jackson hit 'Billie Jean', and her own song of the hour, 'Umbrella'. This was a two-person performance, though, and the artist alongside her would soon become a central character in her life story. His name was Chris Brown.

4.

The Price of Fame

A brutal irony of fame is that someone who is so well known and admired, even loved, by millions of people can feel painfully alone. For Rihanna, this was not a problem in the earliest years of her fame. Back then she was, she told *The Sunday Times*, 'on an adrenalin high' for some time. While she was, as a solo artist and mostly single woman, alone from the start, she never let that trouble her, such was her excitement over these new experiences. 'But after a while, it got repetitive and that's when you kind of go, "Oh wow, I'm sitting in a hotel room once again, me and the television"'.

The *Sunday Times* journalist presented an image of the Caribbean star trapped between the 'guiding hands' of her handlers from behind the scenes and an army of flashing cameras and pushy fans in front of her, concluding: 'Neither seems especially comforting.' Indeed, for Rihanna many of the experiences of fame were frightening rather than comforting. She recalled standing on the red carpet at showbusiness events, the photographers calling out her name so she would turn towards them. For many who dream of international stardom, it is moments such as these that represent the pinnacle of fame.

Yet the reality can be bitter: a tearful Rihanna spoke to *The Sunday Times* of how much anger she sensed in the photographers as she stood before them at red-carpet events. Moreover, once the applause and acclaim had calmed down for the evening, she would often sink into despair and loneliness as she came down from the natural 'performance high' that such events induced. She did not expect floods of sympathy from readers. Indeed, she acknowledged that to everyday members of the public, her position must have seemed trouble-free and enviable. Yet she was learning that, behind the success, 'there are dark sides – there's loneliness, unhappiness'.

Not for the first – or last – time in her life story, it would be a fear of being alone that transported Rihanna to a bad place. She said her requirement for a man was, at its most basic level, simple: he needed to be fragrant. 'A guy that smells good,' she replied when asked by entertainment news show *Access Hollywood* what was most important in a potential partner. 'If I see you and you look good, chances are you won't turn my head. I will look away . . . but if you smell good, I will whip my neck around!' More than anything, though, she needed a man to address the pain and loneliness she was increasingly feeling.

Unfortunately, the man she hoped would be the answer to her loneliness instead caused her new and more painful issues, issues that would continue to plague her in the years ahead.

Born in Virginia in 1989, Chris Brown began performing as a child, singing in his church choir and

(*above left*) With her mother and grandfather at *Time* magazine's 100 Most Influential People in the World Gala, 2012. (*above right*) At the 54th Annual GRAMMY Awards in 2012 with her father Ronald and her brother Rajad. (*left*) Mother Monica Fenty – 'one of the strongest women I know'.

(*above left*) Rihanna shares a special bond with Jay-Z, who signed her to his label Def Jam in 2005.
(*above right*) In concert in Michigan, 2005.
(*below*) After a whirlwind few months, Rihanna earns her place alongside RnB royalty, including Destiny's Child and Usher.

(*above left*) Fresh-faced
and fun-loving: backstage
with Chris Brown at the
Jingle Ball in 2005.
(*above right*) Performing
at the same event.
(*left*) Stepping up the
sassiness at the last
ever Smash Hits Poll
Winners Party in 2005.

(*right*) A girl like me: striking a pose in St Michael, Barbados before the release of her second album. (*far right*) On tour with Jay-Z in Melbourne, Australia. (*below*) Performing in her trademark pink in 2006.

(*above*) Rihanna showcases her ever-changing style as she promotes her third studio album, *Good Girl Gone Bad*.
(*right*) Performing her first Hot 100 number-one single, 'SOS'.

(*above*) You can stand under my umbrella-ella-ella: performing the song that propelled her to superstardom.
(*below left*) Clutching her award for Best Rap/Sung Collaboration for 'Umbrella' at the 50th Annual GRAMMY Awards.
(*below right*) Winner of Video of the Year and Monster Single of the Year at the 2007 MTV Video Music Awards.

(*above*) With Adam Levine of Maroon 5 in 2008.
(*right*) Backstage at the 2006 MTV European Music Awards with Kanye West, with whom she later collaborated on 'Run This Town'.
(*below*) Performing the charity single 'Just Stand Up' alongside (*l-r*) Ciara, Carrie Underwood, Mariah Carey, Mary J. Blige, Beyoncé and Miley Cyrus.

(*top*) In happier times: with boyfriend Chris Brown at the 2009 GRAMMY salute to Industry Icons.
(*above*) Performing onstage together in 2008.
(*right*) Rihanna and her lawyer attend Brown's court hearing in 2009, at which he pleaded guilty to assaulting her.

entering local talent contests. Having been signed to Jive Records in 2004, around the same time as Rihanna, he released his first album *Chris Brown* in 2005 when he was in his late teens, and a second one, called *Exclusive*, followed two years later. Despite being earmarked in the beginning as a possible future Michael Jackson, from the early days Brown's image was always rougher round the edges than that of Jacko – in fact he was actively marketed as a bad boy.

By 2011, he had released four albums; the fourth, entitled *F.A.M.E.*, landed him his first US number one, and a GRAMMY Award. By then, though, he was not only famous but infamous, thanks to the contentious goings-on in his relationship with Rihanna.

They first became friends in 2005. At the Vibe Awards that year, she introduced Brown's slot, in which he performed his single 'Run It'. He was just sixteen at the time, and Rihanna only a year older. It was the following year when rumours first surfaced that the pair had become more than friends: they were said to have been flirting with one another at the Nickelodeon Kids' Choice Awards.

In 2007, Rihanna attended Brown's eighteenth birthday party, which was held at the ritzy 40/40 club in New York. They were snapped together at the bash, both looking very young and innocent. Later in the year, Brown confirmed that he and Rihanna had flirted, but he insisted that, far from being in a relationship with her, he was in fact 'single and ready to mingle'.

Yet the speculations would not stop, even when Rihanna painted their bond as more of a filial than a romantic one. 'We are best friends, honestly, like brother and sister,' she told *MTV News*. As she told it, their bond was less about romance and more about mutual support and understanding between two people who had so much in common, being the same age and having become famous at more or less exactly the same time. A cute image, but not one that many media folk interested in their relationship believed for long, particularly as the duo continued to be seen together at parties, ceremonies and even going on holidays together. Brown continued the denials, saying that 'I am definitely single' during an interview with MTV. 'I have a close friend, but it's not like a relationship. I'm not trying to settle down. I'm only eighteen, so I'm just trying to live my life and have fun.'

However, the evidence of their interactions with one another made it hard to see them as anything less than lovers. When they got matching tattoos, the cat was halfway out of the bag already. As it turned out, Brown was the first to admit that there was more to it than that. 'Our relationship is growing,' he told the *Mirror*. 'We started off as friends and we're getting a little bit closer now.' Just weeks after Brown hinted that they were an item, Rihanna denied that this was the case during an appearance on *The View*. 'He's an amazing person, but we are not dating,' she said of Brown. 'We're very close friends though. Very, very close.' The public felt teased by these contradictory titbits the duo were offering. The truth was that they were dating, and by the end of 2008 they finally admitted as much.

Brown's manager, Tina Davis, filled in any blanks when she stated that they were so close that 'It got to the point where they didn't want to be separated.' The management of both acts found they had to coordinate the two stars' schedules in order that they could spend as much time as possible together. 'They loved each other so much,' said Davis.

One of the early appearances they made together, when their relationship status was still at the 'rumoured' stage, came at an event held in Rihanna's honour in Barbados. The day after she turned twenty, the star flew back to the island to appear at the 'Rihanna Day' event, organized by the prime minister, David Thompson. She arrived in true diva style, flanked by a bevy of assistants, security guards and policemen – and in doing so, she sent a clear message to any locals who resented her success. However, the fact that so many locals turned up, a large number of them clutching umbrellas as a show of support, was heartening for her. 'I am so grateful and I have never been more proud to be Bajan,' she said. 'I want to thank all of you for coming out and supporting me tonight and my career from day one!'

She performed at the event, but much of the media attention focused on the presence of Chris Brown. Just days before, Rihanna had celebrated her forthcoming birthday along with Brown and other celebrities at Los Angeles' Les Deux nightclub. Among the other stars present were rapper Kanye West and actor Wilmer Valderrama. The revelry was crowned when Brown sang an a cappella version of 'Happy Birthday', direct to his girl Rihanna.

At this stage, the relationship seemed so sweet. Two celebrities, both of whom had found fame early, had fallen in love. The media and public adore a successful celebrity coupling: the likes of Jay-Z and Beyoncé, Brangelina, David and Victoria Beckham have fascinated us for years. On a practical level, there is also much to recommend such relationships that bring together two people who understand the motivations, trappings and the required sacrifices of fame. However, celebrity partnerships can also prove to be toxic affairs. With two large egos and two people keen on the limelight in the relationship, there is often friction and envy.

In the case of Rihanna and Brown, there were also fears that the pair's bond had already gone beyond the loving to the needy, obsessive and dependent. Rihanna would later describe their relationship as an 'obsession'.

Add to the mix the fact that both parties experienced domestic violence as children (as a child, Brown had reportedly sometimes been too scared to go to bed at night, such was the violence in the family home), the potential for things to turn dark seemed ever-present. The first sign of a cloud over the relationship came in the summer of 2008 in the shape of reports, unconfirmed by either party, that Brown had asked Rihanna to wear less revealing outfits, as he was concerned she was attracting too much attention from other men. Six months later, the darkest of clouds would envelop the couple. At the time of writing, it has not entirely lifted.

In February, 2009 took a terrible turn. What was about to happen to Rihanna would shock the world and dominate the headlines for months – and even once it slipped off the very summit of the celebrity news agenda, it remains in its upper reaches to this day. Indeed, in the eyes of many commentators and pop fans, it is this controversy that most defines Rihanna.

The trouble began at the pre-GRAMMYs party. This should have been a happy event, the eve of the big night on which Rihanna would perform and vie for an award. She arrived wearing an $11,000 Gucci dress, and was full of smiles. By the end of the night, she would be in tears, and bleeding.

At the party, she thought she spied Brown flirting with British pop singer Leona Lewis. 'Rihanna saw Chris flirting,' a source told the *Mirror*. 'He and Leona were laughing and Rihanna saw his hand on the small of her back. It was totally innocent but it set Rihanna off.'

It was indeed innocent, but later in the evening, as they walked to his car in Hancock Park, Brown received a text message that outraged Rihanna. Sent by a former lover of Brown, the lengthy message suggested, in lurid terms, that she and Brown could rekindle past passions. On reading the message, Rihanna saw red. She confronted Brown about it, and refused to back down. 'I caught him in a lie, and he wouldn't tell the truth,' she explained later to *20/20* US television host Diane Sawyer. 'So I wouldn't drop it . . . I kept saying I couldn't take that he kept lying to me, he couldn't take that I wouldn't drop it, because obviously his back was up against the wall. The truth was right there in the text message.'

After the warring couple got into Brown's rented Lamborghini, the argument continued. According to police notes, Brown tried to eject Rihanna from the car, but knocked her head against the passenger side window. Then, say the notes, she 'turned to face Brown and he punched her in the left eye with his right hand. He then drove away in the vehicle and continued to punch her in the face with his right hand while steering the vehicle with his left hand.'

Elsewhere in the notes it is alleged that Brown made

a blood-curdling threat, telling her: 'I'm going to beat the s**t out of you when we get home. You wait and see!' A terrified Rihanna, who later explained she had 'fended him off with my feet', then rang her assistant and left a voicemail message in which she said: 'I am on my way home. Make sure the cops are there when I get there.' The detective notes say that Brown then said: 'You just did the stupidest thing ever. Now I'm really going to kill you.'

Then, according to the detective notes, Brown put her into a headlock, at one point even biting her. Rihanna would later say that as he attacked her, Brown 'had no soul in his eyes'.

'Brown resumed punching [Rihanna] and she interlocked her fingers behind her head and brought her elbows forward to protect her face,' continue the notes. 'She then bent over at the waist, placing her elbows and face near her lap in attempt to protect her face and head from the barrage of punches being levied upon her by Brown.' Rihanna later told Diane Sawyer: 'All I kept thinking all the time: "When is it going to stop?"' She continued, 'There was no way of me getting home, except to get out of the car and walk. Start walking in a gown, in a bloody face. So I really don't know what my plan was. I didn't have a plan. That whole night was not part of my plan.'

'Battered and bleeding', she made for a sad sight

as she staggered away from the car. Meanwhile, Brown drove to the police station to turn himself in. A member of the public found Rihanna and called for the police and medical attention.

On waking the next day, Rihanna not only had to contend with her aching injuries and broken heart, but also the fact that, overnight, her entire image had changed. 'I felt like I went to sleep as Rihanna and woke up as Britney Spears,' she recalled later in *Glamour* magazine. All she wanted to do was go home and try to rebuild her life. Yet thanks to the ensuing 'media chaos', she realized this would not be an easy move. 'It was like, "What, there are helicopters circling my house? There are 100 people in my cul-de-sac? What do you mean, I can't go back home?"'

When she spoke to the police, the terrible truth about her and Brown's relationship came spilling out. She told detectives that this was, in fact, not the first but the third time that Brown had been violent around her. During an argument in Europe, she recalled, he had pushed her against a wall. On another occasion, she said, he had smashed the windows of a Range Rover vehicle as they argued.

Now he had actually directly beaten her, and at first there seemed little hope of the couple ever reconciling. The public was in shock over what had happened, with enormous sympathy pouring Rihanna's way when the first photograph of her bruised and bloodied face was published. Subsequently, the story behind the emergence of the photograph raised heckles. Her father Ronald complained that it was 'inappropriate' for the photograph to be made public. Describing the photograph as 'terrible', he told *Us* magazine he felt it was 'sloppy' of the Los Angeles police department to allow the photo to be published. That said, he predicted possible positives to the development, hoping it would help the public to 'grasp the situation a lot better'. He explained: 'It's good and it's bad to see the picture because there's other people who were thinking differently, that [Rihanna's injuries] may not be that bad, just a little spank or a little thing.'

Meanwhile, as the anger grew, there were few official placatory words from Brown's camp at first. At one stage, a rumour was put out that he had taken offence at Rihanna spending time with Justin Timberlake at a pre-GRAMMYs party. His stepfather, Welford Hart, told the *New York Post*: 'When you take off your shoes and beat someone with high heels, that's going to hurt. He reacted and tried to get her to stop hitting him, but she kept screaming.' With Brown himself remaining tight-lipped, few would have thought there could be any chance of the couple getting back together. It seemed that the hottest RnB celebrity couple of the hour would go their separate ways for good, never to reunite.

Yet, just weeks later, they underwent their first reconciliation since the incident. With the world still recovering from the shock over what had happened to Rihanna, there was enormous concern that she seemed to be allowing Brown back into her life. They were reported to be together in Miami, Florida. 'I was angry,' she told the *News of the World*, 'then I got vulnerable.' Beginning to miss her man, she became increasingly susceptible to his overtures that they reconcile. With her birthday on the horizon, he bought her an iPod as a gift. She found herself in Miami, in what Brown described to CNN as like something from Shakespeare's *Romeo and Juliet*.

Yet Rihanna, unsurprisingly, felt differently. However cool she tried to appear on the surface, inside she was boiling with rage. 'Everything about him annoyed me: him being around me, him talking to me,' she said on television later. She reached the end of her tether when she told him, 'We can't do this, I cannot continue to do this.' For now, at least, Brown's hopes of rekindling their relationship were dashed.

The public was stunned to learn that Rihanna had even considered getting back with Brown, and that the police case against him was based more on police evidence rather than hers. However – amazingly, perhaps – he did seem to have his supporters. A considerable number of Brown's fans stood by their man, while famous friends of the rapper remained either neutral or loyal to him. Kanye West told VH1 that he, too, 'makes mistakes in life', and pleaded: 'Can't we give Chris a break?' Ne-Yo, meanwhile, told MTV that he would not take sides in the dispute.

It was only after five months of silence that Brown finally spoke, releasing a 'mea culpa' via a video blog. 'Hi, I'm Chris Brown,' he began. He insisted that it was his attorney who had encouraged him not to speak out, 'even though I wanted to publicly express my deepest regret and accept full responsibility'. He then said that he wanted those watching the video to hear 'directly from me that I'm sorry'. He said that he wished he could 'have the chance to live those few moments again, but unfortunately I can't', going on to explain that he took 'great pride in being able to exercise self-control, and what I did was inexcusable'.

'I have told Rihanna countless times and I'm telling you today: that I am truly, truly sorry that I was not able to handle the situation both differently and better,' he continued. 'I recognize that I've truly been blessed: blessed with a wonderful family, wonderful friends and fans . . . I have done a lot of soul-searching, and over the past several months I've talked with my minister and my mother . . . I have let a lot of people down and I've realized that no one is more disappointed in me than I am. As many of you know, I grew up in a home where there was domestic violence, and I saw first hand what uncontrolled rage could do. I have sought and continue to seek help to ensure that what occurred in February can never happen again . . .' As the two-minute video neared its end, he added, 'What I did was unacceptable – one hundred per cent.' He said he 'hoped and prayed' that people would forgive him, and that people would learn from his mistake. In closing, he expressed a hope that he could become 'truly worthy' to be named 'a role model'. Perhaps the most striking thing about the video, though, was that, for all of Brown's words about his regret, there were few references to Rihanna herself. The sincerity of the apology was rather compromised in the eyes of some by the fact it focused on Brown himself, rather than on his victim. This seeming narcissism, and the delay endured before Brown actually spoke out at all, did little to enhance his public standing. Whether any response would have fully satisfied those angry with him is debatable.

So the wheels of the law continued to turn, and the LA District Attorney's office announced in March that Brown was being charged with two felonies – assault and making criminal threats. He was given bail on condition of a $50,000 payment. In the end, facing up to four years in jail if he was convicted of the charges, he made an agreement whereby he was instead sentenced to five years of supervised probation and six months of community labour in his home state of Virginia. He was also ordered to stay at least fifty yards away from Rihanna for the next five years, except at public events where he was permitted to be as close as ten yards. The judge insisted that Brown's community labour should be every bit as unglamorous as that endured by non-famous offenders. 'I want Mr Brown to be treated the same as any other defendant who would come into this court,' he said. 'That means something like Caltrans [rubbish pickup] or graffiti removal, and a two-week domestic violence programme.'

As for Rihanna, she was, to a large extent, something of a mystery during these months. However, behind the scenes she was quietly getting close to another male music star. Born in Canada, Aubrey Drake Graham is better known by his stage name, Drake. Having first become famous through acting, it was as a rapper that he truly made both his name and his fortune. Having sold over 5 million albums, broken a string of records and won a host of awards, Drake is a major player in the twenty-first century entertainment scene. It was not a serious relationship, more of a gentle rebound. 'It was at a really fragile time in my life, so I just didn't want to get too serious with anything or anyone at that time,' Rihanna later told MTV.

Then she began to date another famous man, NBA star Matt Kemp. 'I have a boyfriend,' she told *Elle*. 'I'm so happy. I feel really comfortable and it's so easy. I have such a chaotic life but at the end of the day, that is just my peace. It keeps me sane, really, talking to him and talking to my family.'

But, as so often happens with celebrity relationships, conflicting schedules soon led to the partnership ending. She admitted to sexual frustration during the months after their break-up. When a journalist who was interviewing her seemed disappointed to not land a scoop about a new partner, she said: 'You think you're disappointed? Try being in this body.' Elsewhere in the *Rolling Stone* interview, she admitted she enjoys connecting with men over Skype. 'When you're alone, and those horny moments come up, pictures can be very handy,' she said.

Rihanna would be linked to several other men in the near future. But, as with a lot of gossip that circulates around her, many of the reports were either fabricated or woefully inaccurate. She has learned to laugh such misconceptions off – most of the time. 'Some, you think are funny – then some get frustrating – then you just start to ignore them,' she told *Concrete Loop*. 'But, every time there's a new one, it hits you like brand new. All over again, its starts feeling funny, then frustrating, then you ignore it. Every time I hear a new rumour, it's like wow – and I just know they're going to keep coming so I have to bear with it and not get too upset. You just have to ignore it sometimes.' She would have plenty of rumours to ignore in the years ahead.

*

Artistically, the drive for reinvention continued: her next album, *Rated R*, would see an entirely new Rihanna releasing material to the world. Since the release of her third album, Rihanna had become an entirely different prospect. Musically, the success of 'Umbrella' and the album it was drawn from had taken her straight to the top table. The Brown assault, too, had played a part in her new stature, giving her even more of an edge. Rihanna told *W* magazine that, while recording her new work, she had found 'the mic was my therapist'. She appreciated that, with the microphone and studio, 'there were no negative comments, no negative energy' – a haven, then, for the troubled singer. Not that the creation of her new album had been taken lightly. She told *Access Hollywood*: '*Rated R* is like a child. It needs a lot of attention and it's a lot of hard work and sleepless nights.' Also mixing the mood was the fact that, for the first time, she had paused for longer than a year before releasing a new album. So, for many reasons, *Rated R* was a keenly anticipated piece of work.

The change of atmosphere was clear from the album's artwork alone. Rihanna explained that she wanted 'to do things that weren't done before', and that she had been inspired in her sleep, a time she often conjures up 'crazy' ideas. The cover image was taken by German photographer Ellen von Unwerth, who specializes in shots with 'erotic femininity'. British artist, film and music director Simon Henwood, no stranger to arty expressions and statements rich with flourish, explained the 'R' logo on the album's sleeve. 'The logo is a two-edge sword (literally),' he told the Arjan Writes blog. 'One side symbolizes strength and the other vulnerability. I designed it as a 3D object first that changes form in rotation as an animation – it forms the logo shape at the end of the loop.'

However, what the world was really waiting for was the album's music itself, as even Henwood happily admitted. 'Everything comes from the music, and this is her most personal album to date,' he said. Rihanna echoed this: 'It [is] really personal,' she told *W* magazine, adding that the album came from her in 'the most authentic way'. She compared the process of making the album to a 'movie, in that when I was making this album, every day I was in a different mood. Sometimes I was pissed off, sometimes I was miserable and every song brings out a different story.'

In the making of the album, she had taken more control than usual. Whereas in the past, she had consciously avoided the temptation to be too 'dominant', she was now much more involved. Those who worked with her were conscious of her change of heart for album four, on which she contributed to nine of the thirteen tracks. Ne-Yo told MTV that in the past Rihanna had been akin to a 'puppet' in her compliance in the studio. He said he had hoped that one day she would grow in confidence and become a collaborator – 'and now I think we've gotten there'.

L.A. Reid banged a similar drum but with even more power, stating: 'The people who work with Rihanna execute what she thinks.' No more, he added, would she be a 'little pop girl that you give songs to'. As for Rihanna herself, she even promised that the album would be 'shocking' for her fan base, adding that she expected them to feel 'intimidated' by it.

All the chatter from Camp Rihanna, then, pointed towards *Rated R* being a significantly new departure for the rising star of RnB. It would need to be, as the longer an artist's career progresses the more the critics and customers demand brilliance and originality. If she felt that the reviewers had been harsh on her in the past, they had been, comparatively speaking, wearing gloves back then. From now on, they would expect even bigger things from her, demanding that she justify her continued presence in the industry.

The album begins with the kooky and creepy short intro track 'Mad House', which makes for an atmospheric, dubstep opener, as well as a knowing nod to the eventfulness of her recent life. It also warned those easily scared to stop listening. The first track proper is 'Wait Your Turn', a super-confident song with equal doses of Caribbean swagger and dubstep, lending it a hypnotizing quality. Rihanna herself described the next track, 'Hard', best, saying it is full of 'arrogance' and 'bragging'. Addressed at any other artists who might be 'aiming' at her 'pedestal', her chorus gives such aspirants short shrift. 'Stupid In Love' is not explicitly about the Brown assault, yet given its title, and its lyrics addressing a man 'with blood on your hands', who told her 'lies', the similarities are obvious.

Elsewhere, the album drifts into rock in the form of Slash's guitar solo in 'Rockstar 101'. A song of bravado and aggression, it grabs the listener by the throat in its first bridge of 'the only thing I'm missing is a black guitar', and never lets go. 'Russian Roulette', in contrast, is a near-sibling to 'Take A Bow'. Here, she is vulnerable and resigned. The placing of 'Rockstar 101' and 'Russian Roulette' next to one another is a fine piece of sequencing, reflective of the contradictory nature of Rihanna herself: one moment she is swaggering, the next sobbing. From munificence to melancholy: welcome to Rihanna's world. The feistier Rihanna resurfaces in 'Firebomb', a track in which she imagines wreaking brutal revenge on someone who has wronged her. Given that part of that revenge involves vandalizing a car, the Brown connection is clear. A similarly ebullient Rihanna is in evidence on 'Rude Boy', in which she dares such men to keep up with her. Yet the pain and vulnerability return in 'Cold Case Love'. It is the power of this song that lingers longest in the memory after hearing the album. The swaggering Rihanna of other tracks is brushed aside by the gentle resignation of this lengthy ballad, with lyrics that all too many women would relate to. It plays out with an instrumental climax reminiscent of the closing titles of a Hollywood blockbuster. Such a fascinating, polished and varied album, *Rated R* was a rallying cry for Rihanna's case to be the queen of RnB; never had she been so regal. Her team awaited the critical and public verdicts.

The *Los Angeles Times* review was noteworthy for not just its positive tone but also its length. To devote around 1,000 words to an album review was in itself a significant endorsement of an act. Ann Powers gave it four out of five stars and based her review to a large extent on analyzing the ways in with the album constitutes a personal statement from Rihanna on the Chris Brown affair. Powers correctly identified a 'maleness' to the work, writing that it tackles 'musical styles historically prone to machismo: hard rock, which Rihanna dons like a form of couture, and dancehall reggae, which she knows well but uses here in new ways'. The newspaper's

East Coast equivalent, *The New York Times*, described it as 'in some ways her most risky' album, 'another step in the evolution of a persona'. Rob Harvilla, of the *Village Voice*, also referenced the search for Chris Brown tie-ins that listeners, and indeed the critics, would inevitably embark upon. *Rated R* was, he wrote, 'doomed to be combed for subliminal references to that horrible situation'. He described the Rihanna of *Rated R* as a 'publicly wounded robo-RnB ice princess vacillating between extraordinarily discomforting vulnerability and hilariously operatic boasting'. Fine and fair words. However, he advised listeners to eschew the temptation to project 'emotional subtext'.

Spin magazine was far less impressed, its critic arguing that Rihanna's voice is seldom 'expressive enough to convey fury'. Referring to the profanity of 'Rockstar 101', he added that she 'mewls so preciously you'd think it was her first time swearing'. *The Washington Post*, too, raised questions over whether her vocal style was suitable for some of the messages the album tried to convey, its reviewer wondering whether she was 'truly seething or just pantomiming ire'. He gave it a thoroughly mediocre score of five out of ten. *Pop Matters* felt that its attempt at seriousness ended up 'falling flat'. It was the *A.V. Club* that kicked the hardest, describing the album's music as 'turgid' and its lyrics as akin to 'excerpts from a therapy session'.

Indeed, making the album had proved to be a cathartic experience for Rihanna following the trauma of the Brown assault and its aftermath. However, suddenly one day in Manhattan, she awoke feeling that she had turned a corner. 'I just knew it was over,' she told the *Mirror*. 'It was a different day – I felt different. I didn't feel lonely. I felt I wanted to get up and be in the world. That was a great, great feeling.'

Not that she could leave the episode in her past. Her A-list stature saw to that, yet for every bitter reminder there was a happy one. She was named Woman of the Year by *Glamour* magazine. 'I am shaking right now,' she told the audience. 'I am so nervous but I am overwhelmed and honoured over this honour to be *Glamour*'s Woman of the Year.' Then, *Guinness World Records* named her the most downloaded female artist of all time in the UK. She also snagged two Barbados Music Awards for Song of the Decade with 'Umbrella' and Entertainer of the Decade.

When she released 'Rockstar 101' as a single, she appeared in the video playing the electric guitar part that Slash had contributed to the recording. She had approached various candidates to fill in for the unavailable Slash on the promotional video, among whom were established guitarists Nikki Sixx and Nuno Bettencourt. Both declined, but Bettencourt suggested that Rihanna herself strap on the guitar for the filming.

After further guitarists turned her down, she decided to follow his suggestion.

Slash, watching the finished product, was impressed. 'The video is way better with her being me than with me being me,' he told *Star Pulse*. 'All things considered, it brings an element of sexuality to it that I probably wouldn't have been capable of,' he added modestly. 'I think it's hot.'

In due course, Rihanna would 'rock out' further when she joined Bon Jovi on stage at an MTV Europe Music Awards event in Madrid. 'Wait,' she tweeted the following day, 'Did I just rock out with Bon Jovi last night?' Exciting times, indeed.

She also went on tour, selling out New York's huge Madison Square Garden. When she performed in Tel Aviv, Israel, Rihanna showed her charitable side by handing a free ticket to all who did community service ahead of her show.

For Rihanna, touring comes with a price. As she explained to *Esquire* magazine, moving from hotel to hotel when on the road is not something she relishes, even when those hotels are of the utmost luxury. Instead, she said, 'I like to stay on the bus. I can sleep, I can shower, I can just pull up right to the venue every day.' She works out regularly on tour, in addition to the exercise involved in the live shows themselves. This is because the touring experience disturbs her metabolism:

'I have a trainer. So, she trains me wherever, whenever.'

Celebrity fitness regimes are commonplace, yet other, more unusual, habits of Rihanna's include cracking her knuckles. She also has some peculiar phobias. 'I hate the sound of metal on metal,' she revealed during an interview with *Rolling Stone* magazine. 'And if something isn't even, it weirds me out – like if my girlfriend hits me on the right side of my butt, it feels numb on the left.' She also sometimes watches the same film over and over. For instance, she once watched the movie *Due Date* eight times in a single week. She is, in keeping with her diva image, regularly very late for appointments – and she owns around 1,500 pairs of shoes.

Backstage at gigs Rihanna goes through a regular routine to prepare her body, voice and soul for the performance ahead. She eats lozenges, steams her vocal chords and then speaks to her vocal coach via Skype. 'We sit there at the makeup table and do warm-ups for about a half-hour,' she explained. 'Then, Jen, my personal assistant slash bartender, brings me a shot that she dilutes with a little something so it's not so harsh, like orange juice or soda water and lime.' The shot, of unspecified minerals, helps prepare her and lessen her anxieties. Sometimes, however, she feels so confident that she even slips into the audience, incognito. 'I put on a really big hoodie and sneak out there,' she said. She is rarely recognized, thanks to her disguise.

Then, just before she is due on stage, she and her team have a group prayer, before chanting: 'Where we at, where we at, where we at!' The chant, Rihanna happily admits, is to help remind her of the city in which she is about to perform – she would be devastated were she to hail the wrong city as she arrived on stage. In the last few seconds, she says a final prayer for herself, and also for the audience. 'I always pray for the crowd,' she said.

During some concerts, she has selected an audience member to join her on the stage. 'The way I pick the person is, whoever I feel doesn't take themselves too seriously, or who I think would be majorly embarrassed about it,' she said. Originally, only girls were invited. Then, as she got more confident, she would allow gay guys, and then straight guys to be selected. In time, she even felt confident enough to invite older men up on stage. After each show she is on a performance high. She and her crew scream, whoop, and jump up and down. To cool off, she usually spends half an hour in just her fishnet stockings. It is an image that many male readers will find intriguing, yet Rihanna admits that at the end of a live show, she does not feel like 'a sexy thing'. She does feel invigorated, though. 'You get off stage, and it's like crying and laughing at the same time,' she said. 'It's hard to turn it off when I leave stage.' These feelings were invaluable to her as she recovered from the Brown assault and its protracted, public aftermath. To be out on stage, giving live performances her all, and basking in the warm glow of the audience's excited acclaim, was a therapeutic experience. It helped her remember that she was loved by so many, albeit by those who did not know her personally.

She found solace at home, too, and devoted a room in her Los Angeles pad to one of her earliest musical heroes – the reggae singer Bob Marley. The room included Marley memorabilia and a huge poster of the man. 'The Bob Marley room is my loungey room, so there's incense burning, there's a painting on the wall of Bob Marley in black and white, which I love,' she told *Contact Music*. 'The rest of the room goes from green into yellow into red, like the Jamaican flag.'

A coffee table surrounded by pillow seats added to the informal atmosphere. There, she could reflect on the impact that the late Marley had on music, particularly from her part of the world. 'He's one of my favourite artists of all time [. . .] he really paved the way for every other artist out of the Caribbean,' she said.

Rihanna has covered two of Marley's songs, including 'Redemption Song', which she sang during an appearance on *The Oprah Winfrey Show*, dedicating it to all those suffering as a result of the earthquake that struck Haiti in 2010. Introducing it, she explained that, as a child, whenever she faced 'a difficult situation', she would listen to 'Redemption Song' for strength. She said she found it 'liberating', and continued to listen to it in difficult times.

Times for her had been difficult of late, of course. But they had been educational, too. 'Just when you think somebody was perfect and that it can't happen to you, it does,' she told the *Mirror*. 'I've definitely emerged stronger after the year I've had. Going through a rough experience like that makes you tougher and to get through it takes a lot of guts. I'm naturally a survivor but it's been hard to say the least. I just tried to live my life but it was hard. I was in the spotlight but for all the wrong reasons. Whereas once it was about my music, now all the attention was focused on what happened to me. It was what I call a big interruption. But then with any big life experience, it makes you more resilient.'

Brown, too, tried to find positives among the waste ground of negativity the issue had cast him into. He told *The Times*, 'It's humiliating, yes, but that in itself is good.' He explained that being 'brought back to earth' is sometimes a very good thing. 'It makes you appreciate anew how lucky you've been,' he said, adding that fame had previously cast him into an 'arrogant realm'.

Ultimately, Rihanna took several positives from the most difficult period of her life. This went beyond putting an optimistic spin on the episode, to feelings of near-gratitude: 'Never a failure – always a lesson,' she had tattooed on her collarbone. This, she believed, would mean that each and every day, as she looked in the mirror, she would be reminded that people only learn after making a mistake.

Her recent tribulations had been played out in front of the whole world, yet she had emerged from their aftermath a stronger and wiser person, and with increased poise as an artist. Things would never be the same again – and to a large extent she was grateful for that. 'As traumatic and terrifying as it was, and sometimes I wish it never happened, my whole life changed in the most amazing way after I went through that,' she told *The New York Times*. Most telling in this statement was that she only 'sometimes' wished she had not been assaulted. 'If I didn't go through that, I swear you would've been interviewing a completely different person.' By filtering the episode through her love of reinvention, Rihanna found solace.

5.

A Change of Direction

The fallout from the Brown assault did not only cloud Rihanna's personal life, it also created dilemmas for her professionally. No sooner had she taken her musical career to new heights than the Brown controversy forced her into a difficult position. However much she would have liked, she could not just will away the memory of what had happened to her. Addressing it in song was always a temptation. Indeed, how better to emerge from the negativity than by immortalizing the harsh realities of domestic violence in a collaborative song that would become a global success? As with 'Umbrella', there would be fortuitous timing for her: such a song had just been written.

Top producer Alex Da Kid said rapper Eminem had always planned to invite Rihanna to sing the chorus to the mid-tempo track 'Love The Way You Lie'. 'I definitely wanna get Rihanna on this,' the rapper had told him. Eminem's team got in touch with her, telling her they had the perfect song for her to guest on. 'They reached out to us directly and they just said, "We have this song and we just think Rihanna would be perfect to sing it,"' she told *E!* She responded that, provided the song was up to scratch, she would be happy to do it, as she 'loves Eminem'. In fact, she felt confident even before the song arrived that she would be excited by it and that Eminem would only contact her if he had something very special on his hands. When she heard the track she realized that it certainly was special; she loved it, too. 'It's really beautiful, and it really stands out,' she said. 'It's a really unique record.'

The song's theme, an abusive relationship, was one that struck a chord for both artists. This gave their duet a poignancy that artists with a happier back-story would simply not have been able to manufacture. 'It's something that, you know, we've both experienced, you know, on different sides, different ends of the table,' Rihanna told *Access Hollywood*. She added that she felt Eminem's song went to the heart of the issue. 'He pretty much just broke down the cycle of domestic violence and it's something that people don't have a lot of insight on,' she said. 'The lyrics were so deep, so beautiful and intense. It's something that I understood, something I connected with.'

Work on the recording was completed quickly. The main track, including Eminem's rapped parts, was recorded and mixed in forty-eight hours in the US. Meanwhile, Rihanna was in Dublin, laying down her chorus part remotely at the Sun Studios. It was all hands on deck. 'So we were mixing it while she was recording it and doing it over the Internet,' said Da Kid. The producer, who had worked briefly with Rihanna in London the previous year, was impressed by her. 'Rihanna was super cool,' he said.

So were her haunting vocals. *The New York Times*

Jay-Z's golden girls: after being compared to Beyoncé
as a youngster, Rihanna is now a star in her own right.

(*above left*) A new look for a new book: signing copies of *Rihanna: The Last Girl on Earth* in 2010. (*above right*) Her collaboration with Eminem, 'Love the Way You Lie', reached number one in over twenty countries worldwide. (*below*) Performing with the rapper at the 53rd Annual GRAMMY Awards in February 2011.

(*left*) Revealing her daring fashion credentials at the GRAMMYs in 2001 (pictured with Justin Bieber).
(*below left*) Born to dance, Rihanna struts her stuff onstage at the same event.
(*below right*) Performing alongside rapper Drake.

(*above left*) Something smells good: at the launch of her new fragrance Reb'l Fleur in London 2011.
(*above right*) Shooting the video for 'We Found Love' in Northern Ireland, which caused some controversy with a local farmer.
(*below*) Performing the same song with Calvin Harris during a surprise appearance at Coachella in 2012.

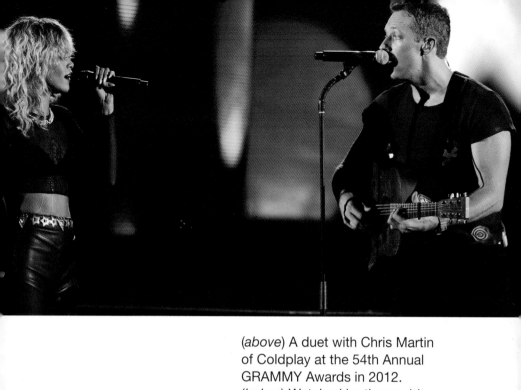

(*above*) A duet with Chris Martin of Coldplay at the 54th Annual GRAMMY Awards in 2012. (*below*) Watched by the world: performing 'Princess of China' at the closing ceremony of the 2012 Olympic Games.

Unapologetic: Rihanna took on 7 countries, 7 days, 7 shows to celebrate the November 2012 release of her new album.
(*above*) At the Kentish Town Forum in London.
(*right*) At Webster Hall in New York.

Retro glamour: a more demure Rihanna at the launch of her fragrance Nude in December 2012.

From ingénue to icon, Rihanna's star has never shined so brightly.

said her contribution 'conveys sadness and regret in a beautifully understated manner devoid of vibrato', while *Billboard* highlighted what it called her 'exquisitely melodic and surprisingly hopeful' singing. However, some press commentators claimed that the duo were, in fact, glamorizing domestic violence. Jenny McCartney of the *Daily Telegraph* wrote that this was part of an unwelcome new trend; a trend she named 'domestic violence chic'.

Upon release in August 2010, the song mesmerized the public, just as it had RiRi. The controversial promotional video also played a significant part in the success. The Barbadian played her role well, sneering as she performed the opening line in front of flames. By the end of the video, following some brutal scenes (played by actors Megan Fox and Dominic Monaghan), Rihanna and the rapper stand in front of a burning house. The expressions she makes as she declares that she 'loves' the way he lies are perfectly poised to puzzle viewers: is she mourning violence and cruelty, secretly revelling in it, or a combination of the two?

The video prompted what seemed like miles of column inches, as commentators queued up to be horrified, titillated or culturally in awe of what it depicted. The song became the soundtrack of the summer across the world, hitting the top of the charts in twenty-five countries. It was the bestselling track of the year in the UK and ended the year in scores of 'best of 2010' round-ups.

Eminem has performed the song live at a string of festivals, often without Rihanna. But at Los Angeles' Electronic Entertainment Expo festival in 2010, he told the audience: 'Before I get into this next song, I wanna bring out a very special guest.' With stunning apple-red hair, Rihanna took to the stage and joined the rapper on their song. Her absence was sorely felt when Eminem performed it alone at the Oxegen festival in Ireland the same month. Before the end of July, the roles were reversed when Eminem appeared as a surprise guest at a Rihanna show at the Staples Center in Los Angeles. In front of a 20,000-strong crowd, she introduced him to a huge ovation.

Perhaps their most emotional live duet to date came in Britain at the V Festival in Chelmsford. Rihanna wore fishnet stockings and a denim shirt for her own set but changed into a black leather dress as she joined Eminem during his. The general consensus of fans and reviewers alike was that this duet was the highlight of the festival. the *Daily Telegraph* called it 'affecting'. Nowadays, when Eminem performs the song live without Rihanna, he unofficially hands her vocal duties to the audience, who happily belt out the words.

A sequel to the song was released, called 'Love the Way You Lie (Part II)'. This features Rihanna on lead vocals, singing the female perspective on the abusive relationship of the original song. It appears on her fifth studio album, *Loud*. Speaking about it to Scott Mills on BBC Radio 1, she explained how she wanted her new album to sound as unique to her as possible. 'I wanted songs that were all Rihanna songs, that nobody else could do,' she said. 'I didn't want the generic pop record that Ke$ha or Lady Gaga or Katy Perry could just do and it'll work. I wanted a song, or songs, that were Rihanna songs, that only I could do, had that little West Indian vibe to it, had that certain tone, a certain sass and a certain energy.'

In themselves these were not contentious words. Any serious pop artist would surely hope that their material would be unique to their talent. All Rihanna had suggested was that she was more determined than ever to put out an album on which her personal stamp was clearly evident. Yet some of the media twisted her words into an all-out attack on Perry, Gaga and Ke$ha. Despite the fact that elsewhere in her Radio 1 interview she had spoken of her hope that she and Perry might collaborate in the future, as far as the media was concerned the Barbadian had opened a military front on her female pop rivals. Rihanna subsequently clarified what she had actually intended to get across with her words, and she is sassy enough to know that a media storm does no harm to the sales of a new work.

Not for the first, nor last, time, she had proved a deft manipulator of the media at an important hour.

The evident re-evaluation of her brand around the time of *Loud*'s release extended to her appearance. Her choice of a new, fiery-red hairstyle was no passing fancy: she very much wanted to stand out from the pack. 'I wanted something that was a new look,' she said. 'Something, again, that wasn't the typical. Black hair is my favourite colour on me. I wanted something that was really expressive and vibrant.' Rihanna was all too aware that the renaissance of female singers in recent times meant she had to up her game.

Rarely had there been so many female solo acts in the upper reaches of the pop charts. At the time of the release of *Loud*, the likes of Adele, Lady Gaga, Katy Perry, Leona Lewis, Amy Winehouse, Dido, Lily Allen and Ke$ha were just some of the female artists going down a storm across the globe. Since day one, Rihanna had been battling to become the number-one female RnB act on the planet. Now, with her sights set ever wider, she wanted to become *the* number-one female act. While her sense of sisterhood made her proud to see such a healthy representation of women in the charts, she still wanted to conquer them all. With her new album she felt she had a fighting chance.

Loud opens with 'S&M', an unforgettable and upbeat tune that captures the imagination in so many ways. First, the fast beat sets out the message that the darker, gloomier atmosphere of *Rated R* is, to the relief of many, not to spill over into this album. Then, the lyrics – 'sticks and stones may break my bones but whips and chains excite me' – hit the listener hard. Whether amused, titillated or appalled, the audience is unlikely to be indifferent. (Rihanna herself audaciously ventured that the song is not quite what people think it is. '"S&M" is not about sex, well it's about metaphorical sex,' she told the *Mirror*. 'The video has lots of whips, chains, dominatrix leather, latex . . .'). It is a bold opener to the album.

The second track, 'What's My Name?', featuring Drake, is as close as she has come to a successor to 'Umbrella'. The song's chorus of 'Ooh na na, what's my name' is equally catchy. She delivers it playfully, with a laid-back Caribbean lilt. So far, so positive. Track three, 'Cheers (Drink To That)', has a party vibe, set to a funky guitar groove, and the next song, 'Fading', is another catchy number. Though it deals with the end of a relationship, it is not downcast but rather serene, and the 'feh-eh-eh-ading' chant of the chorus showcases Rihanna's now-trademark cheerleading.

The anthemic 'Only Girl (In The World)' comes next. This up-tempo, Euro pop song is not just an album peak but a career highlight. Perfect for a club night, it builds gradually to a towering chorus. Never has she sounded so epic. 'California King Bed' is the album's first ballad, complete with gentle guitars and featuring one of the strongest vocal performances of her career. Even at this early stage, the album has proven itself a more varied collection than any of her previous releases.

'Man Down' takes us back, in many ways, to the beginning of her career. The tune has a distinctly Jamaican flavour, while her vocals are more Barbadian. On hip-hop track 'Raining Men', she is joined by Nicki Minaj. It is an off-the-wall song, but its playful lyrics are hard not to love. In 'Complicated', she turns to sadder and more complex terrain. While beguiling, it is nonetheless a track of B-side quality, and a weak spot on an otherwise iconic album. In the smouldering 'Skin', she brings out her trusted dubstep side. Again, her vocals are on top form, blending smoothly with the guitar. The album ends with the aforementioned 'Love the Way You Lie (Part II)'. 'So maybe I'm a masochist,' the lyrics taunt. The ballad take on her Eminem collaboration ends a fascinating album.

No wonder, then, that it was so warmly received. The BBC described the album as 'brilliantly sassy and exuberant at times'. Indie bible the *NME* was, again, approving of the RnB star's work: 'That voice, when she exploits the grit of that Barbadian burr to the max, is more unique and richly textured than ever.' For

The Independent, superficially standout songs such as 'S&M' were of lesser appeal when set against 'the more interesting tracks', which placed 'less salacious demands on her vulnerability'.

Across the pond, where critics are notoriously hard to please, the verdicts had never been so enthusiastic. the *New York Daily News* awarded *Loud* four out of five stars, and praised it as 'effortless and free'. *The New York Times*'s reviewer identified a 'hermetic, cool calculation' at work. He added that *Loud* 'works the pop gizmos as neatly as any album this year, maintaining the Rihanna brand'. The *Boston Times* examined the album in the context of Rihanna's life, speculating that it was as if she were 'liberating herself from the depths' of recent years, resulting in a new collection that is 'all about Rihanna's fighting side'.

For some, however, there were negatives. For instance, *The Washington Post* described the album as 'obnoxious' and 'largely forgettable', defining 'Cheers (Drink To That)' as a 'career lowlight'. But overall the mood was good, with *Rolling Stone* magazine perhaps summing it up the best: 'Maybe the good girl gone bad is getting better?'

Yet it was a wider point that some made at this juncture. Several reviewers commented on the rate at which Rihanna was releasing albums: five in just six years. Given this prolific output was it not time, they argued, for her to take a break, as much for the benefit of the listening public as for herself? Rihanna swatted these suggestions aside: 'You know what? I love making music,' she told the BBC. 'Music is what I do, so I don't feel like there should be a break unless I chose to take a break. There's no such thing as taking a break if you don't want to. I'm here to make music.'

For her fans, this was music to their ears. However, for Rihanna, this determination to remain so professionally energetic came with a price. Indeed, given her wish to emulate some of music's most iconic figures, a break would make sense. Take, in the current era, the commercially commanding Adele. Between 2008 and 2013 she released just two albums, with no fresh release on the horizon as this book went to press. In the same period, Rihanna released four albums. While fans, and some writers, find Adele's slow output infuriating, she manages to keep the public intrigued and desperate for more. (Rihanna is a fan of the British songbird, once declaring of Adele: 'She doesn't know the depth of my affection. She has no idea.')

Not that Rihanna is lacking popularity and commercial success, particularly during the triumphant era of *Loud*. The album reached number one in over a dozen charts across the world, including in the UK, Canada, Ireland, Japan, Norway and Switzerland. Meanwhile, in the US, it enjoyed the strongest first-week sales of any of her albums to date. In the UK, it was the fourth bestselling album of the year, even though it only hit the shops in the penultimate month. It spawned no less than seven singles, each of which fared well. 'Only Girl (In the World)', 'What's My Name?', and 'S&M' were hits across the world, making her a ubiquitous voice on radios, in clubs, bars and anywhere else pop was played.

She also embarked on an international tour to promote the album. The *Loud* tour saw her perform a spectacular two-hour show to audiences in over twenty different countries. She would take to the stage with 'Only Girl (In The World)', a supremely confident selection for a set opener. Yet Rihanna, who would finish with a final trio of 'Take A Bow', 'Love the Way You Lie (Part II)', and 'Umbrella', could afford to push the boundaries. The tour was well received by fans and the media. In total it grossed $90million, making it the twenty-fifth most profitable tour of the year.

Much of the discussion of the concert's set list, as well as the track list of her most recent album, surrounded 'S&M'. Many wondered how true to her life its sentiments were. 'I like to be spanked,' she confirmed during an interview with *Rolling Stone*. 'Being tied up is fun. I like to keep it spontaneous. Sometimes whips and chains can be overly planned – you gotta stop, get the whip from the drawer downstairs . . . I'd rather have him use his hands.' Once, while in Australia, she visited a sex shop in Sydney. She had had a couple of drinks and left the store – called the Toolshed – with two bags stuffed full of sex toys. From this experience she took away a simple motto for life: 'Don't go to a sex store tipsy.' But Rihanna could afford regular retail splurges. In 2010, she was, professionally speaking, doing more than releasing and performing her own music. Her machine was busier than ever. She published a lavish illustrated book entitled *Rihanna: The Last Girl On Earth*. The photographer and 'godfather' of the book was her creative director Simon Henwood. He visually documented a year in her life, as she embarked on her first headline world tour. In a suitably saccharine and adoring introduction to the coffee-table-style tome, Henwood praised her 'effortless style' which, he argued, set Rihanna aside from the 'trying too hards' at the Paris fashion shows to which he accompanied her. He admired her work rate, yet added that she lived much of her life 'with a relaxed Barbadian stride'. The book itself aims for an almost cinematic tone, its title based on a post-apocalyptic dream that Rihanna herself had, in which she wakes up as the only person in a world that has turned into a shrine to her. Fashionista Alexander Vauthier provides a brief preface, which declares that Rihanna has 'the kind of aura that makes one be'. Deep, no?

*

In 2010 Rihanna collaborated with rapper Kanye West on his star-studded ensemble single, 'All Of The Lights'. In it, West sings about serving a prison sentence for 'slapping my girl'. Other guests on the single included everyone from Elton John to Fergie and Alicia Keys, so the reference was almost certainly a mere coincidence. Nevertheless, this was a reminder of how disturbingly prevalent domestic violence is in modern music, particularly hip-hop.

Away from work, she also took on the task of organizing the hen night – or bachelorette party – for singer Katy Perry, who was preparing to tie the knot with bad-boy British comedian Russell Brand. Rihanna was unconcerned by her friend's decision to marry the wayward Brand, whose past included self-confessed addiction to class-A drugs. 'Actually, he's awesome,' she said of Perry's fiancé. 'Even before, when she told me about them two, I was just like "Duh, it makes sense. What took that so long?"' With her blessing on their union firmly in place, Rihanna was asked by the couple to arrange Perry's pre-nuptial girls' bash. Rihanna joked that this was an enormously time-consuming gig to take on. 'It's taking up way more time than my tour,' she said. 'It's so much pressure. Her wedding is probably going to be the best wedding I've ever been to and now

I have to match the bachelorette party to that.'

Yet, when it came to Perry's wedding day in India in October 2010, Rihanna was nowhere to be seen. Various rumours circulated over her absence, including suggestions that she had fallen out with her boyfriend Kemp, and that their row had meant she missed the big day. Rihanna herself said her absence was due to work commitments, and that she had missed it only with a heavy heart. 'I was crushed,' she said. 'I was really looking forward to it, but she understood.' She explained that with *Loud* so close to release, she had to be on call at all times to deal with last-minute queries and issues. With Perry choosing a remote area in India for the wedding, this ruled Rihanna out: 'The album is coming out in two weeks, and I had to be available for a lot of approvals [and check] e-mails and stuff,' she told MTV. 'We couldn't get any phone service or Internet service out there. It was scary.'

Although initially Rihanna was only in the loop over the details of the wedding ceremony via the media rather than direct from Perry herself, she insisted that her friend understood why she had missed the big day and there were no hard feelings, telling *Access Hollywood*: 'Luckily she's in the same industry as me so she understands how it can get, but I was fortunate enough to throw her bachelorette party, so I got to be involved somehow.' She has since quipped that whenever she introduces friends to the stunning Perry, they usually ask her how the star keeps her flawless looks. 'Does she drink the blood of virgins?' is a regular theory they put forward.

While her friendship with Perry endured, Rihanna was about to sever a significant professional relationship, as she parted company with manager Marc Jordan and signed with Jay-Z's Roc Nation. According to the *New York Post*, she and Jordan went their different ways after a disagreement over her 2010 tour. Simultaneously, she announced the launch of a new company entitled Rihanna Entertainment, which a statement to the press explained 'merges all of her businesses, including music, film, fragrance, fashion and book ventures'.

Jay Brown, president and one of the co-founders of Roc Nation, laid down the gauntlet for Rihanna's immediate future, describing her as being in the position of moving 'from being cultural to iconic'. He added that, under his management, she would be encouraged to confound expectations. 'It's good for her to do her own thing and not do the norm and stretch a little,' he told *Billboard* magazine.

Jay-Z was delighted to have Rihanna under his wing. Another major music industry figure who had designs on her was *X Factor* boss Simon Cowell. He desperately wanted her sassy, opinionated and glamorous presence as a judge on his show as it was launched in the US. At the time of writing, Rihanna has yet to succumb to the sweet overtures of Cowell to become a full-time *X Factor* judge, but she has dipped her toe into his televisual pond on two memorable occasions. In the 2010 final of the UK show, subsequent winner Matt Cardle performed a duet with her on the song 'Unfaithful'. After singing the first verse and chorus alone on the stage as is customary, Cardle then introduced the star turn, saying: 'Ladies and gents, it is my absolute pleasure and honour to introduce to you, tonight – it's Rihanna.'

As 'flames' appeared at the front of the stage, which was bathed in suggestive red light, the two stood provocatively close to one another as they sang successive lines. By the end of the song they were as close to each other as possible without actually locking lips and bodies, making it a memorable *X Factor* moment. Cardle later admitted that he had been tempted to move in for an actual peck, and that, as the tension had built between them, he had prayed he would not get an erection. To prevent this he took to imagining Margaret Thatcher, he told MTV. This aside, there was little doubt that Rihanna had pushed Cardle, the eventual champion, over the finishing line. His victory was all the more significant coming as it did in the year that boy band One Direction were among the finalists. The band, which sang a reworked version of 'Only Girl In The World' during the live shows, went on to spectacularly outshine Cardle after the series ended.

During the same weekend final extravaganza, Rihanna also gave a solo performance of her new single, 'What's My Name?'. It was this performance that would really get the public talking – due in the main to what she wore. In fact, it would be more accurate to say that it was what she did *not* wear that caused most chatter. In a performance almost universally reported in the media as 'raunchy', she appeared wearing a black-and-white-striped robe, which she subsequently surrendered to one of her male on-stage entourage, leaving her wearing a strapless bra, high-waist pants and very little else. She delivered the song's bawdy lyrics with what seemed like extra passion and edge. It all made for a risqué appearance on a family show. When chirpy host Dermot O'Leary joined Rihanna on stage following the song, he noticeably kept extra physical distance from her, perhaps feeling uncomfortable standing too close to such a scantily clad beauty.

Her performance and attire polarized viewers: some were enthralled, others were appalled. She was not the only act to prompt complaints that weekend: there were also outraged protests about the similarly adult act put on by Christina Aguilera. Commentators, too, joined in, with the director of the Mediawatch-uk charity saying: 'I don't think it was suitable for a pre-watershed broadcast, I think that's quite clear.' The headlines sparked by the controversy did Rihanna little harm and an artist as canny as her will have known, perhaps even revelled in, the fuss her outfit – or lack thereof – would cause.

The 'scandal' clearly did her no harm in the eyes of *X Factor* guru Simon Cowell, though. The following year, he invited her to appear on the debut series of *The X Factor USA*. Her role this time was to assist L.A. Reid at the judges' houses phase of the series. She was relaxed and comfortable as she joined Reid on a pair of white leather armchairs. It was a lovely moment for her, to sit beside the man who had given her her first record deal. She had more than repaid his faith, as was evinced by her presence alongside him as he weighed up potential new stars. When fourteen-year-old rapper Brian Bradley cheekily told her that, come what may in the competition, he would one day 'do a collab' with her, she could not help but giggle in appreciation of his cheek. After his performance she told Reid that Bradley was '*so* cute', and that she was 'still trippin'', over his talent. When Phillip Lomax performed one of her own songs in front of her, she declared the contestant 'very charming'. She was less impressed with Nick Voss, and wondered aloud to Reid whether perhaps Voss had been stronger in earlier rounds.

Overall she showed the charm and attention to suggest she could be a successful full-time *X Factor* judge in the future. However, given the time investment required for such a role, one wonders if she will consider it an attractive prospect, however much Cowell continues to entice her. In December 2012, in the wake of the end of a disappointing year for the UK show and on the brink of the climax of the US version, Cowell was said to be even more determined to hire Rihanna. The UK show in particular was floundering, and he felt she would be just the person to enliven the franchise in 2013. 'As well as bringing an aura to the panel thanks to her current standing in music, she is also feisty and will make great TV,' a source told *The Sun*. 'Simon loves these sort of characters.' (There was speculation that Cowell, who has a longstanding tradition of holidaying in the Caribbean over the winter, might approach the Barbadian himself.)

*

In November 2011, Rihanna was back doing what she does best: releasing exciting new music, this time in the form of her sixth studio album, *Talk That Talk*. It had been heralded by the single 'We Found Love', which she put out in September. Written by Calvin Harris, it became her eleventh number-one hit in the US, and also topped the charts in many other countries, including the UK. With its electro-pop synthesizers, it is another instantly catchy tune from the Barbadian. As such, it is also an inherently polarizing song: people either succumbed to its addictive nature, or deeply resented it. *Rolling Stone* fell into the latter camp, describing it has 'half-baked' and declaring it 'the worst single of Rihanna's career'. Many artists loved it enough to cover it, though, including Coldplay, Jessie J – and a seemingly never-ending procession of *X Factor* hopefuls on both sides of the Atlantic.

The filming of the single's promotional video turned out to be an eventful and, usefully, headline-grabbing experience for Rihanna. She travelled to Belfast and the filming included the shooting of a key scene in a field that belongs to Alan Graham, a farmer in his sixties. The farmer, who owns sixty acres of land near Bangor, County Down, had never heard of Rihanna until he received a call asking if she could film on his land. 'Someone explained she was as big as it gets as far as pop stars were concerned,' he told the *Daily Mail*. 'I am a bit illiterate about those issues.' He was about to receive a crash course in those issues. As word spread, long lines of traffic built up around the Ballyrobert region as drivers slowed down in the hope of getting a glimpse of the star. A crowd of pedestrians also swarmed as close as they could to the field, with schoolchildren brandishing mobile phones to take photographs. Yet, as the scene went on, she stripped down into skimpier degrees of undress, culminating in a topless scene.

Graham, meanwhile, was out in his tractor in a neighbouring field. Seeing the topless Rihanna, he was shocked and offended. He immediately demanded that they stop filming on his land. 'It became apparent to me that the situation was becoming inappropriate,' he told the *Belfast Telegraph*. The topless scene had, he explained, contradicted his 'ethos'. Later, he explained his decision. 'If someone wants to borrow my field and things become inappropriate, then I say, "Enough is enough",' he said. 'I wish no ill will against Rihanna and her friends. Perhaps they could acquaint themselves with a greater God.'

It became a talking point across the world. On BBC Radio 2's *Jeremy Vine* show, a journalist from the *Belfast Telegraph* complained that Graham's actions had tainted all of the Northern Irish people as backward. A caller to the show expressed a fear that the Rihanna row would damage tourism to Belfast. Yasmin Alibhai-Brown, in a major piece in the *Daily Mail*, jumped to Graham's defence, arguing that Rihanna's sexualized image demeaned all women. The controversy certainly claimed column inches.

Nor was the fuss about the video only focused on its production. When it was finally released, it sparked various complaints that it sent out disturbing messages to viewers. Of particular concern was the scene in which Rihanna is featured being spanked by a man, with the words 'Mine' tattooed across her backside. The Rape Crisis Centre spokesperson Eileen Kelly told the *Daily Star*: 'Rihanna's new video is a disgrace. It sends the message that she is an object to be possessed by men, which is, disturbingly, what we see in real violence cases.'

This row about her video started just days after one about a previous video had been resolved, when she settled a lawsuit with fashion photographer David LaChapelle over the video for 'S&M'. Rihanna settled out of court with the snapper after he claimed some scenes from the video were plagiarized from his shoots. 'I like RiRi,' he told the *Evening Standard*. 'This is not personal, it's strictly business. Musicians commonly pay to sample music or use someone's beats and there should be no difference when sampling an artist's visuals.' The case was settled with an undisclosed sum, and LaChapelle's spokesperson said he was 'happy with the settlement'.

And these are not the only videos of hers that have caused controversy. The filming of her single 'Man Down', on location in Kingston, Jamaica, opens with Rihanna shooting the male character, and then moves backwards in time to portray the events that led to this – the suggestion being that she was raped. As the video was on the brink of release, Rihanna gave a hint that it covered contentious territory when she said: 'We need to be authentic.' She then addressed female viewers of the video via her Twitter page, writing: 'Young girls/ women all over the world . . . we are a lot of things! We're strong, innocent, fun, flirtatious, vulnerable, and sometimes our innocence can cause us to be naive! We always think it could never be us, but in reality, it can happen to any of us! So ladies be careful and #listentoyomama! I love you and I care!'

Then, the fuss really broke out. A spokesperson for the US-based Parents Television Council said that Rihanna had wasted an opportunity of telling young people that, should they become a victim of rape or domestic violence, the most important thing is to seek help. 'Instead of telling victims they should seek help, Rihanna released a music video that gives retaliation in the form of premeditated murder the imprimatur of acceptability,' said Melissa Henson.

Industry Ears, a US organization that monitors the media for disturbing or harmful material, went further. Co-founder Paul Porter said that, in thirty years of monitoring, he had never come across 'such a cold, calculated execution of murder in prime time'. Rihanna responded to the fuss on Twitter, reminding the world that she was 'a twenty-three-year-old rockstar with no kids. What's up with everybody wanting me to be a parent?' In the years ahead, she would often mourn the fact that people expected bland conformity from her; she had never promised anyone that.

Voices supporting Rihanna emerged, including that of a rape victim who had tried to shoot her attacker. She said that the video 'did a great job of getting the entire world to talk about rape'. The *Popjustice* website declared that 'It is not a pop star's job to babysit kids,' echoing Rihanna's own sentiments well. In part, the fuss had been down to the fact that Rihanna exists in the era of social networking websites. On sites such as Twitter, everybody is invited to have and share an opinion on everything, and it is all too easy to complain. She had encountered a fonder response to an intentional PR stunt when, the previous month, she had travelled to her concert at London's O2 by public transport. With her security entourage watching carefully, she happily mingled with the passengers and posed for snaps alongside them as she rode London Underground's Jubilee Line. It was a great bit of public relations as she kicked off her tour. She even swiped her own Oyster card as she passed through the ticket barrier. She has since travelled on the Underground on other occasions, including to attend a Drake concert – for which she cut an extra spectacle by wearing thigh-high leather boots and hot pants – and to a rehearsal for the BRIT Awards. She loves to joke about Oyster cards, correctly identifying them as a cultural benchmark for Londoners.

What of the album itself? The mainstream mood of 'We Found Love' was a fairly decent harbinger of what was to come on *Talk That Talk*, which is, in the main, her most middle-of-the-road effort to date. It also gives the impression of being a somewhat hurried creation, with less direct input from Rihanna herself. The cover features her suggestively staring at the camera and licking her upper lip. Significantly, it also marked the return of the spiky 'R' logo, which had been rested for *Loud*. But, when compared to its successful predecessor, *Talk That Talk* fell a tiny bit short.

'You Da One' barely sets the adrenalin pumping with its staccato lyrics. As an opener it is thin, though Rihanna has stuck up for it, saying: 'It's a sweet little love letter. I love that it has that reggae vibe, but it also has that little bit of dubstep. It's kind of dirty. I love it.'

'Where Have You Been', produced by Calvin Harris, does raise the interest level and sounds magnificent in a club atmosphere. Following the aforementioned 'We Found Love' comes the album's title track. 'Talk That Talk' is a fine tune, enlivened no end by the rapping of guest Jay-Z. For many, though, the album's highlight comes in the form of 'Cockiness (I Love It)', a cheeky little song of twists, turns and several surprises, not least the lyrics: 'Suck my cockiness/Lick my persuasion'. Bombastic, batty stuff, it is followed by the equally risqué 'Birthday Cake' and the cheeky 'Red Lipstick'.

Elsewhere, *Talk That Talk* is a hit-and-miss collection. 'We All Want Love' feels unfinished, which is a shame as a more considered take on it could have produced a career highlight. 'Drunk On Love' samples The xx, but is otherwise unmemorable. A hint of dancehall rears its head for 'Roc Me Out' and 'Do Ya Thang' also has a Jamaican flavour. 'Watch N' Learn' is another highlight – a rhythmic attention-grabber of some urgency. The exquisite vocals of 'Farewell' are partially compromised by a cluttered backing track. Of a similar tempo to 'Umbrella', it is nevertheless forgettable when compared to her signature track. 'Fool In Love', the closing ballad, partially redeems this but is nothing compared to the stature of the closing track of *Loud*, 'Love The Way You Lie (Part II)'.

A mixed bag of an album, then. The same can be said of its critical reception. The *NME* described it as 'annoyingly safe', and suggested 'it may be time for Ms Fenty to take a holiday'. *Slant* went even further, dubbing it 'pretty easily the worst Rihanna album yet'. *AllMusic* rated it higher, but not highly enough, saying it was 'her third best album to date'. The *Los Angeles Times* felt she had pulled her lyrical punches with an eye on Middle America: 'For all the innuendo and introspection, *Talk That Talk* contains little sweat, slobber or fluids and a lot of plasticized, inflatable insinuation.'

Meanwhile, in the UK, the *Daily Telegraph* awarded

her 'adrenalized behemoth' four out of five, praised her work rate, and concluded: 'The whole album is essentially a collection of could-be singles. That might become overwhelming – but with hooks as irresistible as these, it's difficult to care.' the *Guardian* gave the same starred rating, and said the album showed 'exactly why she's at the top of the pop game'.

Despite these differences in opinion, most reviews agreed that *Talk That Talk* was a tamer affair than its predecessor; it was just that some approved of that and some were less keen. The BBC's conclusion that it is 'showy but soulless' was not an uncommon one. *Talk That Talk* debuted at number three in the US, though it hit the top of the hit parades elsewhere, including the UK, New Zealand and Austria. In Britain, it was the tenth bestselling album overall in 2011. With millions of albums sold since the start of her career, Rihanna's success rate remains remarkable.

*

Rihanna is increasingly focused on projects separate from her main musical pursuits. In recent years, she has branched further out to a number of non-musical fields, including fashion, cosmetics and film. In November 2011, she launched her new fashion range. The line, for which she teamed up with huge brands Emporio

Armani Underwear and Armani Jeans, comprises denim and lingerie garments. The launch garnered instant attention when *The Sun* claimed that she used a body double for scenes in the advertisement to promote the Armani jeans. The advertisement features her in bed, clad in lace underwear, and writhing around in the throes of a nightmare. She then rises and slips into a pair of jeans. According to *The Sun*, the raunchy close-up shots of her getting into the jeans in fact featured not her behind, but that of a model named Jahnassa Aicken. It pointed out that the figure in the close-up shots seemed fuller than that of Rihanna, and reported that Irish model Aicken had been spotted by Rihanna's management during the filming of the promotional video for her single 'We Found Love'.

To say Rihanna was unhappy about the report would be an understatement. She fumed on Twitter: 'Ok @thesunnewspaper, this is the only way I could say this to you!!! F**K YOU . . . AND yo baggy ass condom.' She then sent a follow-up tweet asking: 'Who is Jahnassa.'

She could afford a smile when the advertising campaign for Armani was voted the sexiest of the year by the experts of US magazine *Advertising Age*. 'It's Rihanna at her sexiest,' purred the copy. 'She's never looked this good,' they said, adding: 'She's in amazing shape and the pictures are stunning.' That felt better. She was happier when she judged a fashion show on UK television, explaining how she was 'excited to follow the journey of our aspiring contestants and see how their individuality influences their efforts during the course of the show'.

Then came her march into cosmetics: the first fragrance she launched was Reb'l Fleur. The advertising campaign included an unforgettable billboard image of Rihanna sitting naked, her arms and legs covering her modesty. One such billboard was placed in the centre of Times Square in Manhattan. It certainly captured the imagination of the New York masses. Rihanna stated of Reb'l Fleur: 'My new fragrance is about taking control but still being a lady. There's a feminine, romantic element to the fragrance – but there's also a defiant quality in it. I love its duality.'

Her next fragrance, called Nude, was launched in October 2012. Revealing the first advertisement for it on Twitter, Rihanna wrote: 'Make sure you smell sexy, especially naked, this fall.' She later told her followers that the fragrance smelt like 'Me!!!' and said she chose its name because 'it means u don't need to wear anything else.' She told *Women's Wear Daily*: 'When creating my first scent, Reb'l Fleur, I wanted it to be a really strong scent – daring and bold. I have gotten more personal with Nude.'

For much of the media, it was the fragrance's name that was of most interest. Given that on her new album cover, a *GQ* photo shoot, the advertising campaign for a number of products, and a host of topless Instagram photos all featured her either nude or apparently so, people could have been forgiven for forgetting that she ever wore clothing. Even the Tony Duran-shot advertising campaign for Nude, in which she at least wore minimal lingerie, was ruled as 'too hot' to be featured in most department stores. A second shoot was arranged so a less revealing version could be placed in stores. As the promotional campaign wore on, Rihanna continued to wear very little, and, in December, she posted a series of near-naked Instagram images of herself sitting by a fireplace. The photos were shot by her friend Melissa Forde, and were captioned: 'Sneak peak new photoshoot @rihanna #MTFphotography'.

At the launch, which was held in the Beverly Hills branch of luxurious US department store Macy's, Rihanna wore a demure white dress, described as 'virginal' by one newspaper. With it, she wore a bold and gold choker necklace, designed by Christian Lacroix. It was thought to be a gift from Chris Brown, as she had tweeted a close-up of her wearing it, with the caption: 'He told me "you better not give it away."'

Rihanna also developed her cinematic career, appearing in *Battleship*, Peter Berg's epic sci-fi movie, based on Milton Bradley's successful strategic board game. She had received a few scripts prior to that of

Battleship, yet it was only this one that sufficiently interested her. The alien invasion adventure film also featured Taylor Kitsch, Alexander Skarsgard and Liam Neeson in its cast. Rihanna appeared as Petty Officer Cora 'Weps' Raikes, a feisty weapons expert. She looked absolutely stunning on the big screen, not least because in many of her scenes she wore a fetching naval uniform, and was often alluringly wet from the sea spray. That said, far from merely trading on her looks, she had not taken a lazily obvious route back into cinema. As *Total Film* magazine noted, she 'admirably avoided the token hottie role'.

Still, her role was not the most challenging. One website described it as 'a veritable master class in one-line utterances.' On set, she found she had something in common with her character: she enjoyed handling and firing the heaviest of artillery. 'The one on the boat was so powerful, on the ribs, every time, ugh, I remember,' she told *The Sun*. 'I would come back to the set with black gunpowder everywhere – it was crazy. But it was so much fun. I loved it, every moment. I loved feeling it in my chest.' Indeed, she had been amused when she learned that the crew had hired an artillery expert to help her understand how to handle the weapons. She told them she had been 'weapons trained' in the cadets as a teenager.

So, filming was not proving as a big a challenge as

she had feared and she had experience of sorts to draw on. As well as her role in *Bring It On: All or Nothing* back in 2006, she had also acted in numerous music videos in recent years. However, she said the pop video experiences were only of minimal use to her when filming for a full-on movie blockbuster. 'For me, acting was a whole different world,' she told MTV. 'We make mini-movies with music videos, but there's always a song track that's playing, you don't have to speak, so [with acting] you have to tell that emotion with the tone of your voice, and I have an accent, so I had to change it to a bit of an American accent for this movie, so that was different.' For inspiration she studied the work of several actresses. 'There were a few – I won't name them, but there were a few,' she told *MTV News*. '[They were] mostly actresses I looked to and looked up to and embodied their characters and tried to see how they would approach the action. I watched a lot of bad bitches,' she smiled.

Although she had done her 'homework' about acting, she found in the end that she had to learn on the job. She did so with decent speed. She was rather nervous before shooting some of the scenes, but she was soon grinning from ear to ear and telling her co-stars: 'I can see why you love this job.' Her ease on camera was in part down to director Peter Berg, who fed her the lines only very shortly before she had to deliver them. He was keen to avoid her over-thinking or over-preparing, so opted for a more natural approach.

Unable to rely on her natural energy, Rihanna drank a lot of the Red Bull energy drink between scenes. 'This was usually because of the hours,' she told *Interview* magazine. 'It's really weird. On movies, you usually start your days early, like at around 5 a.m., and then you finish around 5 p.m. or 6 p.m., and then, on *Battleship*, which we shot in Hawaii, the time difference was just . . . I was really jet-lagged. I just wanted to keep my energy up during the day. I didn't want to be lazy or feel groggy, so I just kept drinking Red Bull.'

With the drink perking her up, she enjoyed the prank-filled atmosphere on set. Her presence was appreciated and enjoyed, including by her co-star, Liam Neeson. 'My God, she's so cute and she's great in the film,' he said. He admitted he is familiar with her musical work. 'I know her songs well. I've been known to hum "We Found Love" from time to time.'

As for Rihanna, she had been 'in love' with Neeson having watched other films of his in the past. She was so star-struck when she first encountered him on set that she dared not even look at him. It was Neeson who asked whether he could be photographed alongside her for his son. She also enjoyed the presence of Alexander Skarsgard: 'Oh my god, he's so hot!' she said.

The positive verdicts on her abilities from her co-stars were encouraging. Taylor Kitsch was put right on the spot when he was asked whether he felt Rihanna was a better singer or actor. 'Oh, man. This is a tough one,' he said. 'This is intense. She's better at acting.' As for the film's director, Peter Berg, he was glowing in his praise of her thespian skills. 'She was great,' he told the *Daily Mail*. 'She has a very strong part. I was surprised no one had ever thought to hire Rihanna. I was a huge fan of her videos.' Berg has a track record of hiring musicians and turning them into actors. He was determined to hire Rihanna for *Battleship*: 'Obviously she's sexy, but she had this real intensity. I'm like, "Someone's going to get her."'

Just before the movie's LA premiere, Rihanna was rushed to hospital. As soon as her Twitter account went quiet for a while, her fans began to worry about what had happened to her. She answered the growing concern by tweeting a photograph of her arm wrapped in IV tubes and needles. Word was then put out that she was suffering from 'exhaustion' and 'flu-like symptoms'. Luckily, she recovered in time to attend the premiere, and appeared magnificent in a draped white frock which revealed plenty of her back. To say it had a low neckline would be an understatement. 'I'm a lot better now . . . I had a couple days to rest and re-hydrate,' she told *Access Hollywood* on the night.

Commercially, however, the film struggled, failing

to attract a healthy number of young cinema-goers, and also finding it tough going in cinemas up against films such as *The Dictator* and *Avengers Assemble*. As the BBC pointed out, *Battleship* was the worst ever US opening box-office flop compared to the size of its budget. However, away from the US it did fare better.

As for Rihanna, she had loved being part of a film. Immediately prior to the Chris Brown incident, she had been 'heading into focusing on acting, and that got derailed', a management team member disclosed to *W* magazine. Once the initial dust had settled, she began work with an acting coach and got 'serious about it'. In the future, she hopes to act more, and has not ruled out steamier parts, including those involving sexual experimentation. 'I'd love to be an assassin – either that or a lesbian. Maybe both!' she told the *Mirror*. 'Hey, a gay assassin, there's nothing hotter than that. Megan Fox would play my girlfriend – hands down. She's yummy. She's hot.' The critical verdicts did not help the fortunes of *Battleship* at the box office. The *Daily Mail* set a not untypically brutal tone, giving it a mere one star out of five and saying it deserved to 'sink without a trace'. *Entertainment Weekly*, describing it as *'Pearl Harbor* with greater intelligence', kicked off the commentary on Rihanna's role, saying: 'We appreciate the pop culture traffic jam that has musical glam girl Rihanna passing muster as a tough (yet cool!)

fellow sailor.' The *San Francisco Chronicle* slammed her dialogue, while the *Chicago Tribune* delivered faint praise: 'What you might not foresee is that Rihanna, playing a weapons expert, doesn't embarrass herself as an actress; she neither hits the heights of Mariah Carey in *Precious*, nor the depths of Carey in *Glitter*, but her work is perfectly serviceable,' it said. The *Detroit News* said that the film wasted her presence, sniffing that she did 'little beyond blasting guns big and small'. The *Village Voice* described *Battleship* as Rihanna's cinematic equivalent of Chris Brown – and indeed it was he who continued to feature far more in her personal life.

6.

The Rebel Flower

As 2012 progressed, the Chris Brown factor continued not only to define but almost overwhelm Rihanna's public image. She was, it should be noted, largely complicit in this. Whether by design, or merely as a despairing response to the media's incessant fascination, Rihanna increasingly focused on Brown herself, teasing and horrifying the public by slowly welcoming the 'bad guy' of her life story back into the plot. There had been a number of significant developments between her and Brown during 2011, which between them set the stage for their sensational reunion in 2012.

In January 2011, there had been a rumour that the two were dating again. Although a representative for Brown denied the story, regular reports on the pair followed. The next month, a Los Angeles court reduced the severity of the restraining order on Brown, downgrading it to a level-one order. This meant that, legally, the couple could speak to each other once again, as long as Brown did not 'harass, annoy or molest' her.

Any hope from Rihanna or Brown that this would prove a mere legal technicality, and that the issue would remain firmly in the past, were dashed in March, when Brown reportedly went ballistic live on television when asked about the assault. He was appearing on the landmark *Good Morning America* show to promote his new album. In keeping with a number of celebrities, he wanted the slot to be purely about plugging his new product, and was uncomfortable when anchor Robin Roberts steered the conversation to the Rihanna bust-up. As Roberts raised the issue, she touched Brown's leg in a placatory manner, and remarked on how pleased she was that he was relaxed about discussing the story. It was a masterpiece of manipulative interviewing: pre-emptively telling her interviewee how impressive it was that he allowed discussion of a sensitive story, before he had even shown his willingness to do so. For the interviewer, this was a no-lose ploy: even if Brown reacted angrily, it would only make the exchange even more compelling.

Live on television, Brown had been backed into a corner, and uncomfortably tried to steer the conversation back to his material. 'I mean not really, it's not really a big deal to me now, as far as that situation, I think I'm past that in my life,' he said. 'Today is the album day so that's what I'm focused on. Everybody go get the album.'

But Roberts was in no mood to back down and, with further leg touches and reassuring smiles, continued to press the assault issue. Brown, clearly agitated, batted the issue away again. 'This album is what I wanted to talk about, not stuff that happened two years ago,' he said. 'The music enables me to escape and reach my fans. I couldn't care less what anybody else thinks.'

Then, he performed his song 'Yeah 3x'. He was also

due to perform a second track for online viewers, but he refused to do so, furious that the Rihanna issue had been raised live on air. According to reports, including on *ABC News*, he then ripped his shirt off, confronted a producer and smashed the window of his dressing room. Photographs of the smashed window were published in the media. He then emerged, shirtless, on the streets of Manhattan.

After the interview, he sent a bullish, defiant and rather childish series of tweets. He wrote: 'I don't say s**t to anybody and everyone feels its cool to attack me. GROWN ADULTS!!!! that s**t happened three years ago! [. . .] MY MUSIC DOESNT PROMOTE VIOLENCE nor will it ever!' Roberts, too, tweeted about the incident: 'Sure has been an interesting AM @GMA.'

Within hours, a calm-looking Brown was out on the streets again, visiting the Opera Gallery, on Spring Street. However, the media's gleeful reporting of the alleged explosion behind the scenes at *Good Morning America* was far from calm.

Over the course of the rest of the year, further things happened to bring the two stars closer to one another. For instance, they began to follow one another on Twitter. This development, quickly noted by eagle-eyed fans, prompted users to send messages of concern to Rihanna. She responded to the concern, writing: 'It's f****n' Twitter . . . calm down.'

Nevertheless, by the middle of 2012, the two parties were closer than they had ever been since the 2009 bust-up. Rihanna seemed ready to forgive him, yet her feelings were not mirrored by the public. In fact, the closer she got to him the angrier her fans seemed to become. Brown remained defiant. When he won a GRAMMY on the third anniversary of the assault, there was a flood of protests from viewers who felt it inappropriate to honour a man they considered disgraced.

When he became aware of the protests, Brown was far from conciliatory. 'HATE ALL U WANT BECUZ I GOT A GRAMMY Now! That's the ultimate F**K OFF.' Rihanna responded to the fuss with a tweet of her own, in which she pointedly quoted and commented upon lyrics from her song 'Hard': 'They can say whatever, Ima do whatever . . . No pain is forever. Yup! YOU KNOW THIS.'

For the remainder of the year, the Rihanna/Brown saga would be played out on social networking sites, and such online statements were not going to endear the public to either of them, so some more considered public relations work was needed. Rihanna, clearly, was better suited to front this than Brown. During an extensive, intimate interview with Oprah Winfrey, Rihanna spoke candidly of how she and Brown had rebuilt their trust in one another and still 'love each other'. She added: 'The main thing for me is that he is at peace . . . I'm not at peace if he is unhappy or he is still lonely. I care. It actually matters that he finds peace.'

Brown, at this stage in a relationship with aspiring model Karrueche Tran, had nonetheless built bridges with Rihanna to such an extent that they had become 'very, very close friends' again. Rihanna told Winfrey: 'We've built a trust again and that's it. We love each other and we probably always will.' She continued: 'That's not something you can change. That's not something you can shut off, if you've ever been in love.'

Given Brown's relationship with Tran, Rihanna admitted her 'stomach drops' when she saw him, and that she tried to keep her feelings hidden. Speaking about their 2009 bust-up, Rihanna became almost more reproachful of herself than she was of her assailant. 'It was embarrassing. It was humiliating. I lost my best friend,' she said. Of the aftermath of the scandal, she said: 'I was resentful. I held a grudge. I was dark.'

Indeed, she revealed that following the assault she was actually concerned for Brown's wellbeing. 'I just felt like he made that mistake because he needed help. And who's going to help him? Nobody's going to say he needs help, everybody's going to say he's a monster, without looking at the source. And I was more concerned about him.' She added that she was often reminded of Brown by 'the slightest things', and that she missed him.

These were carefully measured words from a woman who knows when to be precise with the media, and suggested a future together for her and Brown. Yet she also sent out contradictory messages. For instance, during an interview with *Harper's Bazaar* magazine, she seemed to be putting barriers up between herself and any prospective partner. Acknowledging she is 'rebellious' in her work, she stated that she is nonetheless 'conservative' in her love life: 'It's pretty much non-existent. If I come across someone who I find really cool, I'll hang out. But the minute I find that we're getting too close I just . . . I don't let people in.'

So far, so ambiguous: yet she came to the brink of directly speaking about Brown as she added, 'When I was in love, I fell so hard . . . The way it made me feel was priceless. And in a blink of an eye my whole life changed. Everything that I knew was different. I never thought I'd feel that pain in my life. I'm afraid of feeling that again.'

On other occasions, she seemed less philosophical and measured and more provocative. For instance, she was photographed apparently kissing her controversial former lover at the MTV Video Music Awards at the Staples Center in Los Angeles. There had been feverish speculation ahead of the ceremony as to whether or not Brown would attend, and, if he did, whether or not he and Rihanna would indulge in a reunion gesture.

Brown, who appeared with bleached-blond hair, took home two awards from the ceremony, but it was his kiss with Rihanna that made the headlines the following day. Within weeks of the kiss, Rihanna was spotted out and about with Brown in New York. First, they were both seen emerging from Rihanna's hotel. Although they exited ten minutes apart, eyebrows were still raised. Rihanna looked sensational, wearing a black mini-skirt and a sheer shirt, which suggested that she was going braless. Her black high-heels revealed black nail polish on her toes. Later, a photograph was taken of Rihanna and Brown at a concert, in which his arm was – depending on which report you read – wrapped around the lady herself, or merely the back of her chair.

Where did this leave his relationship with Tran? Brown confirmed in October that he had split from Tran and suggested that his continued friendship with Rihanna was a factor in the break-up. 'I have decided to be single to focus on my career,' he said in a bizarre video he posted online. 'I love Karrueche very much but I don't want to see her hurt over my friendship with Rihanna.' In the same video, filmed in grainy style in the back of a car, he said: 'When you share history with somebody, then you tend to fall in love with somebody else, it's kind of difficult.' It was an eccentric short video but its message was fairly clear. After he had posted the video online, Karrueche posted a tweet that read, simply: 'Bye baby.'

With his ex-girlfriend out of the picture, Brown was free to rejoin Rihanna. Celebrity watchers could hardly believe what was happening: two lovers who had been embroiled in one of the biggest scandals of 2009 were now, seemingly, on the brink of a fresh start. The hunt for the first official proof was on. A video taken at a Beverly Hills party then emerged in which, for the first time, they confirmed their reconciliation. They looked very fond and comfortable. A source who was at the party said: 'They kissed a few times and were holding hands for a minute. He made sure he claimed her and made her feel comfortable. He was a gentleman – don't worry. He made sure he was by her side the whole night just like when they first met back in the day.'

Rihanna's father Ronald also got involved in the soap opera. Many onlookers expected him to be anxious and angry at the thought of his daughter welcoming Brown back into her arms. Yet, in an interview with *In Touch* magazine, Ronald seemed to endorse the return of the errant Brown. 'I know they love each other. They always have,' he explained. 'She's happiest when she's around him, and as long as she's happy, I am happy and the whole world should be too.'

This was no aberration: he had also told *Grazia* magazine that he and Rihanna's fans considered his daughter and Brown to be 'the perfect couple'. To many fathers, Ronald's words would seem perplexing. But he pre-empted any backlash: 'I think everyone makes mistakes and they shouldn't be held to them forever,' he said. 'Everyone should be forgiven once. There's a lot more to Chris than the whole world knows.' Ronald went on to attribute enormous 'charisma' to Brown and to state that he felt Brown had 'so much respect for me'. He added: 'That's what I love about him. He's always shown me respect.' If only, some readers might have felt, Ronald was more concerned about the level of respect Brown had shown his daughter.

With the entire saga such an increasingly attractive story for the media, high prices were offered for any photograph or report on the subject. Other celebrities were approached for their own take on developments. Oprah Winfrey described how Rihanna had appeared in their recent interview 'with a big, wide, open heart and that she was in the space of forgiveness'. The television icon added that if Rihanna was happy to reconcile with Brown, then she herself had 'no judgement'. Beyoncé, though, was less optimistic about the future. She reportedly told her husband Jay-Z that she felt Rihanna was 'beyond saving'.

The media's obsession with the story snowballed. Soon, a photograph of Rihanna talking on her mobile while on the street was enough to spark a news story in itself, together with fevered headlines wondering whether it might be Brown, the putative villain of the piece, with whom she was speaking. A story that amounted to no more than 'Rihanna phones someone who might be Chris Brown' was actually given column inches. More of a scoop perhaps was when she and Brown were both spotted in St-Tropez at the same time. Despite denials from both camps that Brown had joined her on her yacht, and an insistence from Brown's camp that he was only in St-Tropez to film a music video, it all seemed more than a coincidence.

In due course, Rihanna stoked the embers of the Brown story via her social media presence, often seeming deliberately provocative. First, she tweeted a photo of Brown lying on a Bart Simpson-duvet-covered bed, with the caption: 'Dis n**ga....... #BartObsessed'. She also alluded to Brown, whose tour was called the Carpe Diem tour, when she tweeted: 'All alone in my big ole jet!!! See u soon lover... Happy Thanksgiving everyone... #Berlin #Carpe Diem.' The couple were reported to have spent Thanksgiving together. Then she posted a photograph of her embracing a man who was generally assumed to be Brown on her Instagram account. 'F**kyopictures i dont wanna leave!!!' she wrote alongside the image. 'Killed it tonight baby!!!' Then, she posted another photograph which she accompanied with the x-rated caption: 'Home is where the c*ck is.'

These teasing glimpses of an apparent reconciliation sparked a multitude of disapproving comments among online chatterers. How, they wondered, could Rihanna possibly go back to a man who had beaten her? Soon, these feelings bubbled over when US comedian Jenny Johnson sparked a war of words with Brown via Twitter. The much-discussed argument started after Brown tweeted a photograph of himself with the caption: 'I look old as f**k! I'm only 23 . . .' Johnson replied, 'I know! Being a worthless piece of s**t can really age a person.' Read by millions of tweeters, the conversation continued, with an increasingly lower tone, until Johnson wrote a summary message to her followers:

'Okay. I'm done. All I got from that exchange with Chris Brown is that he wants to s**t and fart on me.' Later, Brown suggested that Johnson ask Rihanna herself 'if she mad', sparking Johnson to suggest he 'get some help'. She added, 'I have zero respect for a person who seems unapologetic for the terrible crime he committed and shows no signs of changing.'

TV star Elisabeth Hasselbeck said of the exchange: 'I think it's disgusting, first of all. But also, it seems like verbal rape to me.' It was a sentiment shared by many, and over the following hours, Brown received waves of abuse from thousands of tweeters, horrified by his unapologetic attitude to his past misdemeanour. This continued until he deleted his Twitter account. As for

Rihanna, her only comment on Twitter was to ask: 'How does one find the time?' adding: 'We gotta do better than this!!' The spat had Twitter abuzz for days.

Yet what the episode had shown more clearly than anything was that Brown was very much on the defensive. So easily goaded into a war of words, the events of 2009 obviously remained a sore point. Just months earlier he had been involved in a nightclub brawl in Manhattan, after which he had published a photograph of his injured face. Onlookers told the media that the fisticuffs had started during a row about the Rihanna assault.

Unofficially, Rihanna was said to be 'distraught' over the quarrel. An insider told *Hollywood Life*: 'She clearly doesn't want anyone fighting and especially not over her.' Only later did she herself make an on-the-record yet ambiguous reference to it, while dining with a magazine journalist. 'There's no proof of that being for my love,' she told *GQ*'s Jay Bulger. 'That's my answer to that question.' Mischievously, she then asked Bulger: 'You ever have bitches fight over you?'

Meanwhile, the events of 2009 were apparently immortalized in a tattoo that Brown unveiled in the autumn of 2012. The inking, on his neck, appeared to be a depiction of a woman's battered face. It inevitably brought back memories of the haunting image of Rihanna after the 2009 assault. Sources close to Brown insisted this was not the case, and that the similarities were just coincidental. They claimed the image in fact depicted a skull associated with the Mexican celebration of the Day of the Dead. Not many were convinced by these denials and most critics could not help but wonder at the tastefulness of a tattoo of this nature, given Brown's past. Then, both Rihanna and Brown got such similar tattoos that it could only have been intentional. Brown's was of a fighter jet, while Rihanna's was of a bird woman. But their overall designs were eerily alike.

Just when the public thought it had heard everything it could about the pair, jaws dropped again when, in the same month, Rihanna tweeted a message of support to Brown ahead of a court hearing to determine whether he had violated the terms of his probation for assaulting her. 'I'm praying for you and wishing u the best today!' she wrote. Brown responded: 'Thank u so much'. As the Twitter community recoiled in shock, Rihanna sent a follow-up tweet: 'Praying for you baby, my best wishes are with you today! Remember that whatever God does in our lives, it is WELL DONE!!! #1Love'.

Just days later, the media was reporting that former Pussycat Doll Nicole Scherzinger was spotted canoodling playfully with Brown at Supperclub's Black Diamond Pyramid party in Los Angeles. Brown's representatives denied the two were anything more than good friends, yet this would not be the last time in the year that he would be spotted partying with other women. With Rihanna seemingly accepting Brown back into her life, and her father and several celebrities apparently giving the reconciliation their blessing, the public were craving a hero who would step in and advise her against such a seemingly reckless path. Jay-Z was rumoured to have warned Brown that, should he harm Rihanna again, his career would be over. However, Jay-Z's knight-in-shining-armour stature was denied by Brown himself, who said that no such threat had been made during their recent conversation. 'It was cordial. It was real respectful,' Brown told US radio station Power 106. 'It was nothing like that. Me and him, it was like a green room [situation] and it was cool. People like to take it and run with it because they have nothing else.'

At the beginning of December, Brown showed that while he may have left Twitter, he was still willing and able to use online social media to stir up debate. 'What would music today sound like if [Rihanna and I] didn't exist?' he asked his followers on Instagram. Uncomfortably, several respondents suggested it would sound better, with one commenting: 'It would sound like real r&b.'

Such words did not seem to hurt him. Within days Brown was back on Twitter, posting a photograph of himself and Rihanna, with the caption: 'What would music today sound like if these kids didn't exist?'

As for Rihanna herself, she reportedly denounced Katy Perry as a 'hypocrite' after the singer condemned Brown and Rihanna's indulgence of him. Rihanna was said, by *Star* magazine, to feel that Perry was in no position to criticize her, as her own partner John Mayer 'is one of the biggest sleazeballs on the planet!'

Meanwhile, Rihanna remained focussed on her appearance. Just months earlier she had spoken disparagingly of her much-envied physique. 'I'm working on getting my butt back,' she said. 'It used to be my favourite body part, but now it's disappeared! I'm going to have to start hiking or at least going on the elliptical or walking on an incremental treadmill or horseback riding. Something that firms the butt.' Rihanna had long feared the decline of her backside and her chest, telling *Rolling Stone* that 'butt and tits' are always the first to go. While women around the world continued to envy her bum, Rihanna felt it could be improved, and she went on to outline how she aimed to address her intake. 'I'm eating everything. I've been eating ice cream and fast food and Italian food. I drink a lot of coconut water. It balances out all the other toxic stuff I put into my body.'

One of her favourite restaurants in the world is Giorgio Baldi in Los Angeles. She is a big fan of their gnocchi and spaghetti dishes. She also enjoys eating in, with a nice glass or two of chardonnay to accompany her own culinary creation. During the winter of 2012 she posted a photo of her drinking Jack Daniel's as she frolicked on an ice rink.

In love, however, she likes to take more of a backseat. For instance, when asked by the American edition of *GQ* what turns her on, she described how she likes the man to take control in relationships. 'I like to feel like a woman,' she said. 'I have to be in control in every other aspect of my life, so I feel like in a relationship, I wanted to be able to take a step back and have somebody else take the lead.' She added: 'Love makes you go places you probably wouldn't ever go, had it not been for love. But I think everybody still has their limits.'

These words, set as they were next to a new passage about her and Brown at a nightclub, raised eyebrows among readers. However, Rihanna was merely playing with the public again. With the mega-selling bondage book series *Fifty Shades Of Grey* the talking point of 2012, she was as much as anything just playing to the atmosphere of the moment.

In December, there were reportedly angry words between the pair after Brown was said to have been out partying with ex-girlfriend Karrueche Tran in Paris. *The Sun* newspaper claimed that Rihanna was furious. A source was quoted as saying: 'She can't get it into her head that Chris will never change. She's given him so many chances since he beat her up in 2009 and he still keeps hurting her by partying with girls.'

The lady herself wrote a catalogue of fuming tweets, each of which was apparently aimed at Brown: 'Examine what you tolerate', 'Goodbye muthaf*****', 'You give, you get, then you give it the f*** back' and 'Claps for the basic b******'. Yet, true to the form of 2012, she soon made up with Brown, posting a black-and-white photograph of her cuddling up with what appeared to be his tattooed arm. She also subsequently deleted her angry tweets, replacing them with a message saying: 'Damn....... I miss my n****'. It seemed that Brown was akin to a cat with nine lives when it came to earning Rihanna's forgiveness.

What many of her fans found difficult about the Brown saga was that Rihanna seemed so unreceptive to their sympathy and offers of support. It mystified them that she would even countenance further dealings with Brown. During an interview with *Rolling Stone*, she attempted to explain how she is drawn towards pain and its sources. 'I do think I'm a bit of a masochist,' she said. 'It's not something I'm proud of, and it's not something I noticed until recently. I think it's common for people who witness abuse in their household. They can never smell how beautiful a rose is unless they get pricked by a thorn.' Warming to her theme, she added: 'When I think about it, I really do take some pleasure in the negativity. I don't want to say turned on by it – but

I'm turned on by it.' These sentiments at least in part explain her continued dalliances, both personal and professional, with the man who had assaulted her. On her seventh album *Unapologetic*, released in November 2012, she and Brown perform a duet on a track called 'Nobody's Business'. Is this a direct message to those who had been so upset over her reconciliation with Brown – a hint that she did not welcome any interventions? During an interview on Facebook Live, she seemed to suggest it was. '"Nobody's Business" is basically the way I look at everything regarding my personal life,' she said. 'You know, even though you have to witness it as being documented at every second, it still is mine . . . this is mine at this point. When it gets to my music and stuff like that, I will give and I'll give and I'll give, and I feel like I just need to keep a little bit for me that I get to decide.' Indeed, it was not hard to read even the album's title itself as being a statement on her reunion with Brown.

7.

Conquering Them All

A fascinating and controversial album, as a project *Unapologetic* was slow to start, but was swiftly concluded. 'I have not started working on new music,' Rihanna said in the early summer of 2012. 'I started working on the new sound, but I haven't really started recording yet.' For once, it seemed, our prolific, workaholic heroine was in no immediate hurry to release a new album. She had other directions in mind, as she explained: 'This year, we kind of left a little room to play in other playing fields like movies, acting, fashion.'

Recording finally began on the album in June, at the Metropolis Studios in Chiswick, West London. Rihanna was in the capital to perform at the Radio 1 Hackney Weekend. These performances would set the tone for the album, reminding all involved in its creation that the songs would need to be suitable for performance in front of huge audiences. 'When I was in London she was performing at a festival in front of, like, 30,000 to 40,000 people,' explained songwriter Claude Kelly. 'So I didn't want small songs that only worked on radio, so I tried to do anthemic big-stadium-themed songs.'

The mission was clear from the start: to produce an album that not only outclassed anything she had produced before, but also to make it her edgiest, most urban-flavoured RnB work. Not that Rihanna wanted the album to be predictable; instead she wanted it to be a number of different styles forming one powerful whole: 'I love experimenting and I love working with different sounds and putting them together so they're not one-dimensional.' Speaking to *GQ*, she echoed the familiar protestations that she was not a pop product, saying that she wanted songs with confrontational sharp edges. Given the perceived presence of Chris Brown in the album's tracks, *Unapologetic* certainly does not lack dimension.

Musically it is a rich and dextrous album, which sees Rihanna working with an array of talented artists, including David Guetta, Stargate, Ne-Yo and Nicky Romero. She left a fine impression on Romero, who spoke glowingly to MTV about how down to earth she was in the studio. 'I remember when Rihanna walked in, she was just in her normal clothes,' he said. 'There was no performance clothes, of course, and she had her friends with her and part of her team. She was really nice and she gave everyone a hug and just very, very polite. It felt like she could be someone from my school or someone I was friends with before. I don't know; she was very, very humble.'

For a star of Rihanna's stature, the most commonplace human behaviour – wearing normal clothes and being polite to your fellow man – can be lauded as evidence of flabbergasting humility. But Romero continued: 'I remember that she was very much like everyone else, very normal and a normal person. I appreciated that someone from that level is being so humble and thankful for her work and for her career.' The key track he had worked with Rihanna on was the dance song 'Right Now'. He played her some hip-hop and dance songs he had worked on, and she was quickly enthusing over what they could make. 'Yeah, I want to have this song combined with that world,' she told him. 'And actually I want both worlds to glue together and make it one thing.'

Not everyone who worked with her on the album was complimentary, however. 'Earthquake' singer Labrinth, who co-wrote and produced her track 'Lost In Paradise', said that it had been 'difficult' and added, with a cheeky laugh, that he 'managed to get through it'. When pressed, he refused to elaborate, saying: 'It was just difficult.' The fact that in the same interview he was eager in his praise of Emeli Sandé and his experiences working with her only added weight to his indictment of Rihanna. 'It was great working with [Emeli] and seeing how our song kicked off,' he said.

This was not the only time Rihanna was accused of being difficult in 2012. She arrived several hours late for an interview with Radio 1 disc jockey Nick Grimshaw. He told *Metro* that the excuse her team offered for her tardiness fell apart when the lady herself arrived. 'Everyone was really apologetic,' he explained. 'They were saying, "Oh she's had a really busy morning, she's been doing promo all day and she's really tired and she's really, really busy. She'll get here when she can."' Then, Rihanna arrived and contradicted this message. 'She came in and just started this yawn and I was like, "Oh hi, how are you? Have you had a busy morning?" and she was, like, "No I've just been watching TV all day",' he said. She was also criticized for reportedly demanding six outfits during her appearance at the station's Hackney Weekend festival.

In October, while work progressed on the album she revealed its title. 'I named my album *Unapologetic* because there is only one truth, and you can't apologize for that. It's honest. I'm always evolving of course, I think the only motto I have is to be true to myself.' As it turned out, work continued on the album right up until thirteen days before its release: the absolute deadline for the final cut had been set as 6 November 2012. Jay Brown hit the deadline, turning it in at 6 a.m. 'If we can record a month later, two months later, all the way to Nov. 6, we're never going to stop until that date,' Brown told *Billboard* magazine. 'We're never content.'

Messages of Rihanna's hard work were widely echoed. Island Def Jam A&R man Abou 'Bu' Thiam, said he had never seen Rihanna so committed in the studio. 'She went crazy, especially with the vocals she cut for these sessions, because she just felt like it would be a really huge record,' he said. 'Nobody had ever heard Rihanna do a record like this. She does all kinds of songs for every album that no one's heard, like "Birthday Cake" or "Man Down", which are great, unexpected moments. We wanted even more of those for *Unapologetic*.' On the album's release, Team Rihanna was at pains to promote her involvement in all aspects of the album's creation. As Jay Brown said, 'She's not here to make a record and take direction. Every record that has ever come she's always changed something.'

The album had been heralded by the single 'Diamonds', which was released in September. It is a mid-tempo semi-ballad, blending pop, soul and electronic styles. It is notably smoother and softer than much of Rihanna's previous output, and as such played well to the market. Vocally, she sounds distinct and throaty. Though some felt it lacked power and thrust, the single sold well, topping the charts in sixteen countries, including the UK, the US and Canada. A remix followed two months later, with Kanye West providing rapped sections.

The album itself was convincing and potent, reflecting the hard work and finesse that had gone into its creation. The first half in particular has a darkness and edge unparalleled in her previous work. 'Diamonds' was always earmarked as a single. As Steve Bartels, president/COO of Island Def Jam Music Group, said of the song:

'It covers four to five different formats in terms of reach – that's the depth of a real superstar.' Another standout track is the hypnotic 'Pour It Up', which was chosen as the album's second single. Its strip-club imagery is stark, and for the cover of the single a topless Rihanna is featured, holding a dollar bill over her mouth. Yet it has also been spoken of as having an element of 'girl power' to it. As producer Mike WiLL said, 'After they hear "Pour It Up", girls won't be scared to flex, won't be scared to talk about their money.'

More controversial is 'No Love Allowed', in which she sings: 'I was flying 'til you knocked me to the floor'. It would be lyrics such as these that would raise eyebrows among listeners and raise questions in the critics' reviews. Rihanna herself, keen as ever to be seen to have creative input into and control over her material, co-wrote four tracks: 'Right Now', 'Phresh Out the Runway', 'Nobody's Business' and 'Love Without Tragedy/Mother Mary'.

The album was released on 19 November 2012. It debuted at number one in both the US and UK. The US number one was her first in the album charts, a huge step for her. In the UK, she equalled Madonna's record of having three consecutive number-one albums and in so doing, she also managed the mighty feat of knocking One Direction off the top of the charts.

The critical response was mostly admiring in its

tone, albeit as much focused on her personal life as her music. A common theme was also how prolific she had become, releasing seven studio albums in seven years. Indeed, she had released an album in each of the past four Novembers, so something of a tradition was being built. Jay Brown was unapologetic about this. 'She's always making music, because she loves it,' he told *Billboard*. 'So the strategy starts as soon as we get the idea for the next album. Are we going to release another album next year? I don't know. But it's just a natural thing for her. She'll say, "I'm going to do a record," and the next thing I do is focus on going on tour.'

As *The Independent*'s critic put it, this left the impression 'that if you flipped up her impassive panel of a face, you'd find circuit boards and wires'. *Rolling Stone* positioned Brown as 'the abusive ex she took back' and 'like a co-writer throughout, sort of the way Germany was a co-writer on World War II'. Of the material itself, it described the 'stark, shadowy RnB' as 'confrontationally honest and sung within an inch of its life'. The *NME*, not known for its overall admiration of RnB, gave it a healthy seven stars, stating: 'At its best, *Unapologetic* trades in daring avant pop.' The review added: '*Unapologetic* makes a compelling case for Rihanna knowing what she's doing.' Coming from a publication so hung up on musical credibility, this was praise indeed.

On the negative side, the aforementioned *Independent* reviewer declared Rihanna's voice to be 'as flat as Norfolk', and judged the overall album as 'dull as dishwater'. Online magazine *Pitchfork* wasted no time in putting the boot in, describing *Unapologetic* as 'turgid' in the first sentence of its review. Several hundred words of damnation later, many of them focused on the Brown factor, it concludes: 'On a track-by-track basis, the songs make for dull labour, not worth our time and not befitting Rihanna's talent.'

The BBC review went surprisingly far given the website's usually measured tones. 'Instead of anything cheeky or fun, this set is laced with the very real presence of someone using the spectacle of pop music to inadvertently condone abuse,' it thundered. Middle Eastern publication *The National*, meanwhile, accused her of 'peddling unsavoury messages through a medium supposed to be light and escapist'.

Harsher still, however, was Eric Henderson writing in *Slant* magazine. He began his review by asking: 'Why should we believe anything Rihanna says anymore?' He then accused her of exploiting the Brown episode, and doing so in a 'disingenuous' fashion. No sooner had she told her audience, he wrote, that it was none of their business than she continued to 'shove it down our throats'. He closed his review with a hope Rihanna might one day understand that 'being *Unapologetic* isn't the same thing as picking fights on the dance floor'. Scathing words indeed.

*

A challenge for Rihanna in the coming years will be to emerge from the shadow of the Brown incident. Cynically speaking, it has not been without its benefits professionally. But, as time progresses, it seems the costs will far outweigh the benefits, so for the sake of her career she may well be tempted to consign it to the past. A cryptic tweet she sent in December suggested she was tiring of Brown. She wrote: 'Never underestimate a man's ability to make you feel guilty for his mistakes.' She also uploaded a photograph of a handwritten letter she had composed to her fans. It contained a few hints at the Brown controversy, its tone suggesting she was approaching closure on the matter. It covered how to deal with what she called the 'curve balls that life can bowl' at one, and 'taking our lessons and growing from them' as well as 'keeping it moving without regrets'.

Yet rumours in December suggested Brown could become a permanent fixture in her future. First, it was reported that she had added a Brown tribute to her collection of tattoos. *The Sun* claimed she had the word 'Breezy' inked onto her body – a reference to Brown, who refers to his fans as 'Team Breezy'. Then, celebrity gossip weekly *Closer* reported that Rihanna had asked her record label when would be the best time to pen in some downtime to her schedule so she could have a baby. A source told the magazine the reaction from the label was one of shock: 'They just stared at her. Everyone was pretty open-mouthed.'

Whether or not this story is true, it is unlikely she will become a mother during 2013, which is already packed full with work commitments for her, and not short of arrangements for Brown. Furthermore, when she has spoken on the record about the prospect of becoming a mother she has discussed it in distant terms. As she told *Interview* magazine: 'I mean, I have a lot of other stuff to accomplish before I get to kids. So . . . Whenever the time is right, I'll just know. I don't really plan on the age.'

But her final word on the Brown saga, as this book went to the press, seemed to indicate their relationship was over. 'Being single sucks,' she posted online. 'The only thing I get to do anymore is whatever the f**k I want to do.'

Meanwhile, to promote her new album she embarked on a gimmicky tour. Entitled 777, it saw her set off on a round-the-world trip in which she would play seven concerts in seven countries in seven days. She invited 150 journalists to join her for the tour, along with a lucky group of fans, who each won their place in a competition. It was an ambitious project, and one that was far from being a complete success. The entourage and Rihanna were exhausted early on in the travelling, as time zones were crossed. Journalists and fans also suffered from jet lag and both complained regularly of a lack of access to Rihanna.

Speaking to Nick Grimshaw on Radio 1, she defended herself: 'It was different having to do your job but also have 200 guests come along with you,' she said. 'They all want you to host a party every time you get on the plane after a show but you really only have that time to sleep until you get to the next country. Sometimes it was a two-hour ride to the next country and that was all the sleep you would get.' Therefore, she said, she preferred preserving her abilities to schmoozing with the media. 'I knew I had seven countries and seven shows and I had to save my voice,' she said. 'I didn't go crazy. I didn't party too hard. I did have fun though. I tried to get everybody involved but sometimes you just wish you could give more.' She also apologized to the fans, in a separate chat with *US Weekly*. 'I had to preserve my health, normally, I'd be back here popping bottles with y'all,' she said. 'I had to preserve my voice. I was worried about my body more than partying on the plane, so I had to just sleep whenever I could.'

With the tour kicking off in Mexico City, it moved to Toronto, Stockholm, Paris, Berlin and London and then ended with a final concert in New York, in which Jay-Z joined her on stage. Kicking off her set with 'Cockiness', she found her way through a host of hits, finishing with 'Umbrella' and 'We Found Love'.

The tour hit trouble in Berlin, in particular, when she arrived late. The audience had been queuing since before 8 p.m. to be in place for the advertised start of 9 p.m. So, when Rihanna did not appear until 11.30 p.m., there was considerable disdain where there should have been excitement. She had also run late in Stockholm.

In Paris, things were happier. She was joined by a number of guests, including P Diddy. She left Le Trianon on the shoulders of her security guards, leaning over to shake the hands of her adoring fans. In London, according to *The Times*, she did not spend enough time actually singing on stage. 'That was the most unapologetic thing: Rihanna wasn't actually singing for much of the time,' complained Ed Potton. He continued: 'You almost admire her chutzpah, but it all made for a curious experience: part audience with a megastar, part marketing blitzkrieg, part laser-splashed club night, with a bit of world-class singing thrown in.'

As a public relations campaign the tour had been novel and not unsuccessful. Having released six albums prior to *Unapologetic*, Rihanna knew she would have to think outside the box to keep the media interested.

Further, more conventional, tours are arranged for the future, tickets having been eagerly and swiftly snapped up by her adoring fans. She is set to tour deep into 2013, taking in arenas, halls and open-air venues fit for large-scale performances. She will join folk band Mumford & Sons on the bill of T in the Park, as the festival celebrates its twentieth birthday.

Rihanna also had special reason to look forward to the 2013 GRAMMYs ceremony – she is nominated in three categories: Best Pop Solo Performance for 'Where Have You Been', Best Rap/Sung Collaboration for 'Talk That Talk' alongside Jay-Z and Best Short Form Music Video for 'We Found Love'. Somehow, the GRAMMYs always loom large in her story. She celebrated the news on Twitter by including her fans in the glory. 'Congrats guys, we got #3 Grammy Nods!!! #ThugLife,' she wrote. She had teased her supporters with an announcement the previous day on Twitter, writing: 'Big news coming tomorrow!'

Meanwhile, her commercial juggernaut rolled on. She overtook Eminem as the most 'liked' artist on Facebook. Just months earlier, the rapper had taken the lead when he reached 60 million 'likes'. Rihanna snatched the title from him in October, when her 'likes' soared almost as high as 62 million. A more traditional milestone was passed when she was named the top Pop Songs Chart artist of the past twenty years by *Billboard*.

This honour is all the more impressive when it is considered that, unlike some of her most prestigious opponents for the title, Rihanna had only been an active commercial act for seven of the twenty years. The thirty-four chart songs she had on the weekly countdown, including nine number ones and twenty-one top-ten hits, put her top of the pile. 'Billboard crowned me #1 top 40 artist of the decade just 7 years into this!!' she tweeted. 'My fans just majorly s**t on ur existence. #HistoRIH.'

Within hours there was further exciting news for Rihanna in the form of her four nominations for American Music Awards, including in the artist of the year category. Only Nicki Minaj received the same number of nominations for the ceremony. With her catchy latest single 'Diamonds' a huge hit across several territories, it even beat the new release from boyband One Direction in the same week in the UK to the top spot. Her popularity is showing no sign of waning and, as long as her heart is in her career, she has a strong chance of the sort of longevity that eludes most artists. Renewed reinventions of her image will help her case and could even push her towards the sort of stature enjoyed by Madonna. 'If I had to examine her evolution through time, I think she reinvented her clothing style and music with success every single time,' Rihanna said of the Material Girl, in an interview with *We Love Pop*.

Commercially, she has already made a conquering success of things. 'Rihanna is a global superstar without equal,' said the CEO of her record label. Yet her ambitions are huge and her hunger and thirst insatiable; she simply adores the attention and riches that come with fame, and will perhaps never be satisfied by the amount she receives of either. What next for this phenomenal artist? Will she seek to branch out from her current paths, and if so, how?

It does seem likely she will take on more acting roles. While promoting *Battleship*, she said she enjoyed the challenge of drama, describing her experience of the filming as 'unbelievable'. She added: 'I love doing movies now. It's something I want to do more of. I just want to pick films that are wise for me and roles that I can pull off, nothing that is too big for me.' There is indeed a tradition of musicians making a successful move into acting, including Barbra Streisand, Kris Kristofferson, Whitney Houston and Mariah Carey. Rihanna has her champions in the industry, though not all praise her in the most sincere of terms. James Bond star Daniel Craig stated that she would make a better Bond Girl than Beyoncé, arguing that he would favour Rihanna because 'she's dirtier'. She has also been considered for roles in other films, including *Fast and Furious 6*. 'There's a whole other chapter ahead,' said a management spokesman of her acting aspirations.

There will also be further forays into fashion. Among the projects on the horizon is a collaboration with British high-street retailer River Island. 'I find London really inspiring and River Island love to have fun with their clothes,' she told *Look* magazine in a suitably saccharine statement. 'I'm looking forward to creating something really special.'

Despite all this, in a 2012 interview with *GQ*, she spoke with more passion about music than she ever had before, so it seems she is unlikely to cast aside her therapeutic microphone. 'I want to make music that's hopeful, uplifting. Nothing corny or super sentimental,' she said. 'I just want it to have the feeling that brings you out of whatever you're going through. I want it to spark that fire. I want it to be real, authentic, and raw.'

These were not the words of an artist who is at all exhausted with the medium, despite the fact she has already released seven albums. She will branch more into other fields, but at the heart of the Rihanna operation will always be music. It has been an obsession since she sang so sweetly as a child in her Barbados home, and then dreamt of becoming 'the black Madonna'. She could not have even imagined that she would make such a crashing success as a pop artist. At the time of writing, she had sold more digital units of her work than any other artist – including The Beatles.

Her influence is vast: it encompasses not only her

music and artistry, but her image and style, too. Even country singer Miranda Lambert, in a chat with *OK!*, acknowledged a debt. 'She is constantly surprising me with her style and inspiring me to break out and try new things,' she said. 'Well, I don't necessarily get inspired by the whole no-bra thing, but I love that you never know what she's going to wear. It always keeps you guessing, which makes her sassy and interesting.' Women around the world are similarly fascinated. The *Guardian* summed the mood up well, declaring: 'Rihanna's wardrobe is the most talked-about, influential and dissected in pop right now' and that whatever she wears 'is immediately reproduced on the high street, because it sells.' Carrie Tyler, the editor of the website for style-bible *Elle*, agrees. She noted that whenever the website publishes an article about Rihanna's style, its traffic 'goes through the roof'. Tyler isolated Rihanna's confidence as her key asset, though she acknowledged it is merely one among many. 'She is a figurehead for gutsy, confident fashion choices,' said Tyler. 'Women are fascinated by her because she takes the risks that her fans would like to take themselves. She's got a beautiful, curvy figure but it's her confidence that appeals as much as her body.' You can't win them all, though. The *Mirror* included her in their round-up of 'epic fashion fails' of 2012, citing her 'stripy pyjama suit with over-sized (as in 10 too big) blazer, which only served to hide her sexy figure, but was probably . . . er, very comfy'.

But she ruled supreme in a raft of positive 2012 round-ups. Her influence as a style icon was recognized by *Time* magazine, which named her on its 'The World's Most Influential People' list. Stella McCartney, who penned the accompanying mini-essay, said: 'She's one of the coolest, hottest, most talented, most liked, most listened to, most followed, most impressive artists at work today, but she does it in her own stride.' McCartney added: 'This is the beginning for Rihanna – she has so much more to do and to give. She is just getting going, so watch out.'

In 2012 she also received the unexpected honour of being named MTV's 'Rock Star of the Year'. Although she strictly stands outside the genre, the video channel praised her 'audacious attitude, salacious singles, extreme excess and downright defiant deeds'. Then, *Billboard* remarkably placed her at number one on its 'Top 40 Pops Songs Artists of 1992–2012' list. To add some context, this placed her ahead of a prestigious pack including the likes of Lady Gaga, Justin Bieber, Adele and Madonna. 'Her accomplishments are exceptional,' reasoned *Billboard*.

She is still so young, yet her legacy is shaping already. Just as Rihanna has aimed to emulate the success and approach of artists such as Beyoncé and Madonna, so might there be budding Rihannas in the years to come.

Indeed, one young artist has already been spoken of in such terms. Rita Ora, who signed to Jay-Z's label, is often compared to the Barbadian. But the budding star largely dismisses the perception. She told the *Guardian*: 'I don't think there will be a next Rihanna. But I think [Jay-Z] definitely sees me as someone who could be as big as Rihanna. She's a superstar now but they first knew her as a small-island girl – and they want to repeat that success.' Despite her careful tone, Ora is clearly delighted to be compared to Rihanna, as well she might be. (Snoop Dogg made a wise observation regarding these comparisons: that unless Ora works *extremely* hard, as Rihanna does, she has no chance of emulating her success. 'Rita can be whatever she wants to be as long as she stays passionate and keeps working hard,' he told *The Sun*. 'Rihanna works hard, you hear me? Wattup, Rih Rih!')

As for Rihanna herself, she is less than euphoric at the weight of responsibility that comes with being a role model, as we saw in her defensive reaction to the media storm that erupted over her video for 'Man Down'. 'See, people . . . they want me to be a role model just because of the life I lead,' she told *Vogue*. 'The things I say in my songs, they expect it of me, and [being a role model] became more of my job than I wanted it to be. But no, I just want to make music. That's it.' Island Def Jam manager L.A. Reid offered a similar picture, explaining that Rihanna is not aiming to become 'a consensus builder'. He added that she is in charge of her artistic and creative destiny, explaining: 'She's not looking to see what the room thinks – the people who work with Rihanna execute what she thinks.' For her, this principle is as much about avoiding future regret as it is having control in the present. 'I don't want to look back at this thirty years from now and say "I did it all to make them happy and I didn't enjoy it,"' she told *Marie Claire* magazine. Rather, she said, she wanted 'to be able to say people loved me because of who I am'.

She increasingly represents a figurehead for those who feel like outsiders in a strange world, yet she shrugs off the 'rebel' tag that she imposed on herself. 'I think the term rebellious is a term society has created for people being themselves,' she told *OK!* magazine. 'A lot of people just aren't like the others and they understand that and they have accepted that, and they are not afraid to be that, and people don't understand that and that's why it comes off as rebellious.' Her poise and self-assurance are growing, prompting deeper levels of self-awareness, which can only provide more stability in the future. Indeed, during an interview with *Esquire* she admitted that she was hurt by criticisms in the past but has since learned to block out the negativity by ignoring all reactions to her activities. 'Who wants to be bashed every day of their f**king lives?' she asked. 'That's not fun. Today I could eat an apple, and ten people like it and one will not. The next day I could do shots and five people will like it and five won't. What's important is, you never know. You can't do it for the reaction because it's never going to be the same. I learned to live my life with the blinders on. At one point it was so bad, it became numb for me. It was a scary place to be.'

Despite her strength, the criticism continues. In December 2012, the influential *New Yorker* magazine declared: 'Her voice isn't particularly compelling; it conveys not emotion, but, rather, a position of powerful detachment. There's so much Auto-Tune applied to her voice that it's hard to say how she does or doesn't sing.' This is a familiar tenor of criticism: it takes us back to the earliest days of her career, when she was presented as a puppet, slavishly doing what her masters told her to, and devoid of any personal spark herself. Many have since revised that perception, but Rihanna knows that she will never entirely shake it off. A number of different factors fuel this perception. First, there is the snobbery which dictates that the world of pop is populated only by pretty but talentless acts. Second, there is misogyny at work that states a woman can be beautiful or gifted – but never both. Third, and here Rihanna is complicit, her image is often one of submission. However, in an interview with *Rolling Stone*, she attempted to draw an important distinction between her public and private power dynamics. 'Being submissive in the bedroom is really fun,' she said. 'You get to be a little lady, to have somebody be macho and in charge of your s**t. That's sexy to me. I work a lot, and I have to make a lot of executive decisions, so when it comes to being intimate, I like to feel like I'm somebody's girl.'

The Barbadian has so many spoils to enjoy. At the end of 2012, she bought a new mansion in the heavenly Pacific Palisades district of California. There is a saying in Los Angeles that describes her new district well: if you're famous you live in the Hollywood Hills, if you're rich you live in Beverly Hills, and if you're lucky you live in Pacific Palisades. That said, other famous and rich people *do* live in the neighbourhood, but they are mostly very grounded celebrities made up of accomplished people living a normal, albeit comfortable, existence. Rihanna moved there after selling her Beverly Hills home, which, despite the 'rich' reputation of its surroundings, had suffered from leaks.

Her new home comprises 11,000 square feet, standing regally within 33,541 square feet of private land. With seven bedrooms and nine bathrooms, it is a true celebrity mansion. It had plush cream and white textiles when she purchased it, though she naturally planned to impose her own style on its interior. No effort was spared to guard her privacy, with mature oak and sycamore trees and a high fence surrounding the property. High ceilings – including a fourteen-foot one in the kitchen – add to the opulence of it all. The grounds have a large swimming pool, complete with fountains and mood lighting, a Jacuzzi, and barbecue area. The garage alone is vast, and can comfortably house four large cars.

She bought a brand new silver Ferrari at the same time, announcing the purchase on Instagram with the caption: 'All I see is signs, all I see is dolla ign.' She was also presented with a Porsche by her management. All in all, the property and its contents are physical testimony to the success of her career to date. Her home and her lifestyle are so much grander than she could have believed possible, growing up as she did in a three-bedroom bungalow on Westbury New Road, Bridgetown. But what ought to matter most is Rihanna's personal happiness. With annual earnings for 2012 alone of $53m (£32.8m), she is a wealthy woman and can afford to take a prolonged break, or even retire. Despite her dedication to her career, there are times in which she wishes to do just that. 'There's some days I would wake up and it's like, I want to hide sometime,' she told *Access Hollywood* in 2012. 'Is there one island where there's no paparazzi, like, where nobody gives a s**t? Like, is there one place like that?' As she had recorded *Unapologetic*, the pressure of the paparazzi had been particularly fierce. They followed her from the studio to her home, and everywhere in between. 'It was too much. I wanted to just work and focus on my work, not have to deal with this and the flashing lights and you know I just, I wanted to just work in a little hole. I just wanted to focus and it was hard to do that. Times like that you think, "Yeah, this sucks!"'

Yet speaking to *GQ*, she insisted the relentless demands of her career are worth it, for as long as she is appreciating her craft. 'Sometimes a person looks at me and sees dollars. They see numbers and they see a product,' she said. 'I look at me and see art. If I didn't like what I was doing, then I would say I was committing slavery.'

So many of those who find fame in their teens go off the rails in their twenties, before quickly disappearing from the limelight. Her controversial and much-discussed on-off relationship with Brown aside, Rihanna shows few signs of any such fall from grace. Yet the tough veneer she presents to the world hides a softer soul. Again, it is the contradictions that loom large. 'I think a lot of people have a misperception of me,' she told *Interview*. 'They only see the tough, defensive, aggressive side. But every woman is vulnerable. They have vulnerability. So of course I'm going to have that side.'

Rihanna has been famous for so long, yet she is still only twenty-five. Having been in the public eye since her teens, she is still finding her real self. 'I'm always evolving, of course,' this complex, fascinating woman told *Women's Wear Daily*. 'I think the only motto I have is to be true to myself.'

Bibliography

Blair, Linda, *Birth Order* (Piatkus, 2011)

Govan, Chloe, *Rihanna: Rebel Flower* (Omnibus Press, 2011)

Oliver, Sarah, *Rihanna: The Only Girl In The World*
    (John Blake, 2011)

Rihanna, *Rihanna: The Last Girl On Earth* (Rizzoli International
    Publications, 2010)

Discography

This is not intended as an exhaustive list of all Rihanna's many releases. What follows is a list of her major releases and their chart positions, together with some interesting side projects.

Albums	UK	US
Music Of The Sun (Island Def Jam 2005)	35	10
A Girl Like Me (Island Def Jam 2006)	5	5
Good Girl Gone Bad (Island Def Jam 2007)	1	2
Rated R (Island Def Jam 2009)	9	4
Loud (Island Def Jam 2010)	1	3
Talk That Talk (Island Def Jam 2011)	1	3
Unapologetic (Island Def Jam 2012)	1	1

Singles	UK	US
Pon de Replay (Island Def Jam 2005)	2	2
If It's Lovin' That You Want (Island Def Jam 2005)	11	36
SOS (Island Def Jam 2006)	2	1
Unfaithful (Island Def Jam 2006)	2	6
We Ride (Island Def Jam 2006)	17	107
Break It Off (Island Def Jam 2006)	n/a	9
Umbrella (Island Def Jam 2007)	1	1

Shut Up And Drive (Island Def Jam 2007)	5	15
Hate That I Love You (Island Def Jam 2007)	15	7
Don't Stop The Music (Island Def Jam 2007)	4	3
Take A Bow (Island Def Jam 2008)	1	1
Rehab (Island Def Jam 2008)	16	18
Russian Roulette (Island Def Jam 2009)	2	9
Hard (Island Def Jam 2009)	42	8
Wait Your Turn (Island Def Jam 2009)	45	110
Rude Boy (Island Def Jam 2010)	2	1
Rockstar 101 (Island Def Jam 2010)	n/a	64
Te Amo (Island Def Jam 2010)	14	n/a
Only Girl (In The World) (Island Def Jam 2010)	1	1
What's My Name? (Island Def Jam 2010)	1	1
Raining Men (Island Def Jam 2010)	1	1
S&M (Island Def Jam 2011)	3	1
California King Bed (Island Def Jam 2011)	8	37
Man Down (Island Def Jam 2011)	54	59
Cheers (Drink To That) (Island Def Jam 2011)	15	7
We Found Love (Island Def Jam 2011)	1	1
You Da One (Island Def Jam 2011)	16	14
Talk That Talk (Island Def Jam 2012)	25	31
Princess Of China (Island Def Jam 2012)	4	20
Birthday Cake (Island Def Jam 2012)	n/a	24
Where Have You Been (Island Def Jam 2012)	6	5
Cockiness (Love It) Remix (Island Def Jam 2012)	n/a	102
Diamonds (Island Def Jam 2012)	1	1
Stay (Island Def Jam 2012)	6	n/a

Collaborations/Miscellaneous

J Statu: Roll It (SRP Recordings 2007)	n/a	n/a
Maroon 5: If I Never See Your Face Again (A&M/Octone Records 2008)	28	51
T.I.: Live Your Life (Grand Hustle, Atlantic 2008)	2	1
Just Stand Up! (Charity fundraiser, 2008)	26	11
Jay-Z: Run This Town (Roc Nation, Atlantic 2009)	1	2
Eminem: Love the Way You Lie (Aftermath, 2010)	2	1
David Guetta: Who's That Chick (Virgin 2010)	6	51
Redemption Song (Charity Fundraiser, Island 2010)	n/a	81
Kanye West: All of the Lights (Def Jam 2011)	15	18
Nicki Minaj: Fly (Universal Motown 2011)	16	19
Drake: Take Care (Universal Republic 2012)	9	7

Picture Credits

Page 1: McMullan Co/SIPA/Rex Features (top left); Lester
Cohen/WireImage/Getty Images (top right); David
Livingston/Getty Images (bottom)

Page 2: Startraks Photo/Rex Features (top left); Paul Warner
WireImage/Getty Images (top right); Kevin Mazur/
WireImage/Getty Images (bottom)

Page 3: Dimitrios Kambouris/WireImage for Clear Channel
Entertainment/Getty Images (top left); Startraks Photo/Rex
Features (top right); Brian Rasic/Rex Features (bottom)

Page 4: Scott Gries/Getty Images for Universal Music (top left);
Kristian Dowling/Getty Images (top right); Startraks Photo/
Rex Features (bottom)

Page 5: Amanda Edwards/Getty Images (top left); Henry Lamb
BEI/Rex Features (top right); Robert Sabo/NY Daily News
Archive for Getty Images (bottom)

Page 6: Chris Polk/FilmMagic/Getty Images (top); Vince Bucci/
Getty Images (bottom left); Ethan Miller/Getty Images
(bottom right)

Page 7: Chris Polk/FilmMagic/Getty Images (top); Kevin Mazur
WireImage/Getty Images (centre); John Angelillo/LANDOV/
Press Association Images (bottom)

Page 8: Rick Diamond/WireImage/Getty Images (top); Kevin
Mazur/WireImage for Clear Channel/Getty Images (inset);
Lori Shepler/AFP/Getty Images (bottom)

Page 9: Lester Cohen/WireImage/Getty Images

Page 10: LANDOV/Press Association Images (top left); Vince Bucci/Picture Group/EMPICS Entertainment/Press Association Images (top right); Lester Cohen/WireImage/Getty Images (bottom)

Page 11: Larry Busacca/Getty Images for The Recording Academy (top); Kevin Mazur/WireImage/Getty Images (bottom left); Jeff Kravitz/FilmMagic/Getty Images (bottom right)

Page 12: Yui Mok/PA Archive/Press Association Images (top left); Peter Morrison/AP/Press Association Images (top right); FilmMagic/Getty Images (bottom)

Page 13: Kevin Winter/Getty Images (top); Peter Macdiarmid Getty Images (bottom left); EMPICS Sport/Press Association Images (bottom right)

Page 14: Jon Furniss/Invision/Press Association Images (top left); Samir Hussein/Redferns via Getty Images (top right); Kevin Mazur/WireImage/Getty Images (bottom)

Page 15: Jason Merritt/Getty Images (main picture); Jon Kopaloff/FilmMagic/Getty Images (inset)

Page 16: Kevin Mazur/WireImage/Getty Images

Lyrics from 'No Love Allowed' copyright Def Jam Recordings, 2012

Index